"Discouragement paralyzes and disables us, and Meyer brilliantly and pastorally addresses the problem and administers the biblical cure. *Don't Lose Heart* is piercingly clear and biblically faithful, and it will give hope and joy to many. An invaluable treasure."

Thomas R. Schreiner, professor of New Testament interpretation and associate dean at Southern Baptist Theological Seminary, Louisville, Kentucky

"From the beginning of this book it is obvious that it was written by someone with a pastor's heart and a theologian's mind. Pastor Meyer offers insightful understanding about what brings us down and what causes us to lose heart at different moments in life. If you are going to look at your past failures, you must look all the way back to the cross, at the foot of which, Jason argues, you may leave any and all your shortcomings. If you are worried about the future, you may as well look all the way forward to see a bigger picture of God, along with a final and grandiose view of the glory awaiting you. The world needs more Jason Meyers . . . pastors who think theologically, are capable of counseling their sheep through their writings, and can competently train the leaders who will walk with them. This book refreshed my memory and my soul."

Miguel Núñez, senior pastor of International Baptist Church, Dominican Republic

"Have you ever considered that discouragement is a liar, telling you half-truths about the world and, namely, God? Jason Meyer's pastoral care and biblical guidance helps us see the truth about discouragement so that we may bask in the goodness of God's grace. In *Don't Lose Heart*, we are reminded of our glorious hope—and it's the whole truth, truth that is sure and will not put us to shame."

Trillia Newbell, author of *If God Is For Us* and *God's Very Good Idea*

"We all get discouraged; we all lose heart. So the real issue is what we do with our discouragement. How do we handle it? How do we fight it? In *Don't Lose Heart*, Jason Meyer doesn't simply tell us to buck up and stop crying. Instead, as the subtitle suggests, he provides *Gospel Hope for the Discouraged Soul* by exposing the half-truths that lead to discouragement and calling us to replace them with the whole truths of who God is for us in Christ. Since we all lose heart from time to time, read this book as a gospel balm for your weary soul and share it with others so that together we may spur one another to believe the whole truths of the gospel, keep heart, and persevere in faith until all our hopes are realized in the new heaven and new earth."

Juan R. Sanchez, senior pastor of High Pointe
Baptist Church, Austin, Texas, and author
of *Seven Dangers Facing Your Church*

"Here is what a kind, wise, godly friend would tell you when you are discouraged. It is good for all of us that these words are written down. They have lifted my heart to Christ and, in God's providence, will lift the hearts of many."

Kathleen Nielson, speaker and author of *Women and God*

"Jason has written a treasure! I love this uplifting book. It encouraged me in heart and mind and helped me love Jesus more. I'm recommending it to everyone I know."

Mack Stiles, pastor of Erbil International Baptist Church,
Iraq, and author of Marks of the Messenger and Evangelism

DON'T
LOSE
HEART

DON'T LOSE HEART

GOSPEL HOPE *for*
the DISCOURAGED SOUL

JASON MEYER

BakerBooks

a division of Baker Publishing Group
Grand Rapids, Michigan

© 2019 by Jason Meyer

Published by Baker Books

a division of Baker Publishing Group

PO Box 6287, Grand Rapids, MI 49516-6287

www.bakerbooks.com

Printed in the United States of America

Library of Congress Cataloging-in-Publication Data

Names: Meyer, Jason C. (Jason Curtis), 1976– author.

Title: Don't lose heart : Gospel hope for the discouraged soul / Jason C. Meyer.

Description: Grand Rapids : Baker Books, a division of Baker Publishing Group, 2019.

Identifiers: LCCN 2018057349 | ISBN 9780801094422 (cloth : alk. paper)

Subjects: LCSH: Consolation. | Encouragement—Religious aspects—Christianity. | Depression, Mental—Religious aspects—Christianity.

Classification: LCC BV4905.3 .M49 2019 | DDC 248.8/6—dc23

LC record available at https://lccn.loc.gov/2018057349

The information provided in this book is not intended to be a substitute for professional medical advice, diagnosis, or treatment of clinical depression, anxiety, or other psychological conditions. Always seek the advice of your physician or a qualified health care provider with any questions you may have regarding a medical or psychological condition. When a doctor's advice to a particular individual conflicts with advice provided in this book, that individual should always follow the doctor's advice.

19   20   21   22   23   24   25   7   6   5   4   3   2   1

To Cara—
my best friend,
love of my life, and
fellow fighter-for-sight

CONTENTS

INTRODUCTION

Why Discouragement Is a Liar

THE BIBLE INCLUDES some stories that seem downright strange. Have you ever read something in Scripture and wondered how on earth it applies to our lives today? The Old Testament book of 2 Kings contains a story so archaic it seems unlikely that we could relate to it nowadays.

At the time the story took place, the nation of Syria was warring against Israel. Every time the king of Syria planned an attack, Israel's king would somehow find out about his plans and thwart them. Exasperated, the Syrian king declared there must have been a spy in his ranks and demanded to know who it was. His servant informed him that there was indeed a spy, but he wasn't from Syria. Instead, the informant was the prophet Elisha, who had been receiving visions of the king's secret plans directly from God and then relaying that information to Israel's king.

As you can imagine, the king of Syria did not take the news well.

One morning, as the prophet Elisha and his servant got up, they encountered a very troubling situation.

> When the servant of the man of God rose early in the morning and went out, behold, an army with horses and chariots was all around the city. And the servant said, "Alas, my master! What shall we do?" (2 Kings 6:15)

Elisha and his servant were going about their regular daily lives when suddenly they were surrounded by one of the greatest armies in the ancient world, the Syrian army. The imbalance of the situation seems almost comical. What were two people against an entire army? When Elisha's servant looked at the Syrian chariots and horses surrounding him, he cried out in despair at their seemingly hopeless scenario.

As we read this story, it's easy to think, "That's interesting enough. But what is the application for me today? I don't have a hostile army forming a siege circle around my home."

You and I may not be staring down an enemy force from a foreign country, but we do face seemingly hopeless circumstances every day. In 2 Kings 6, the dynamics of discouragement are almost perfectly on display. Like Elisha and his servant, we sometimes find ourselves surrounded by difficulties, and that is when the servant's question becomes our question: "What shall we do?" We share the same problem: We are blind to the big picture.

The Danger of Discouragement

Discouragement is a liar, and the danger is that sometimes these lies are hard to spot because of their sophisticated packaging. The distorted lies of discouragement come to us like a wolf in sheep's clothing. They are clothed in half-truths because they only get part of the picture right. Here is where the story of Elisha's servant and the Syrian army makes its most powerful point. The servant was right about the reasons to lose heart. There was an army of reasons to be discouraged—literally! But the servant saw only half the story.

Elisha told his despondent servant to look at their circumstances again. He needed to be confronted with the full truth so he wouldn't be discouraged by the half-truth. Elisha told him,

> "Do not be afraid, for those who are with us are *more* than those who are with them." Then Elisha prayed and said,

"O LORD, please open his eyes that he may see." So the LORD opened the eyes of the young man, and he saw, and behold, the mountain was full of horses and chariots of fire all around Elisha. (2 Kings 6:16–17)

Discouragement can be defeated only when the full truth of everything that is for us confronts and conquers the half-truth of fear and despair. When the full truth vanquishes those half-truths, our hearts will be comforted and strengthened. In other words, we can "take heart."

This is the way the Bible speaks of discouragement again and again and again. It does not pretend that the problems are not there; it simply declares that there is more to see. The Christian life is a fight for sight. If all we see is what is against us, the shackles of discouragement will keep us confined to a prison of despair. When we see that the One who is for us is greater than all that is against us, our chains will fall off and our hearts will be free to hope again. Losing heart is easy when the chains of discouragement close tightly around our hearts and choke our hope. But we can take heart when the chains are gone and our hearts set free once again. Seeing the bigger picture is the key to unlocking the chains of despair.

Seeing the bigger picture is the key to unlocking the chains of despair.

The Dynamic of Discouragement

We lose heart when we believe half-truths because they remind us that there are *real* reasons to become discouraged. Those troubling facts feel compelling when they stand on their own, and it is easy to become overwhelmed by discouragement because the reasons are real.

I have bad news and good news to share. The bad news is that our fallen world is full of many reasons to lose heart, and they are easy to see. It does not take any special skill to recognize the reasons in our everyday lives. It does not take faith to become discouraged. We just have to take a look at some of the problems that plague us. Discouragement is a heaviness of heart that comes from feeling the weight of those problems piling up on us.

Here is the good news: The reasons to take heart are greater than the reasons to lose heart!

But here is the good news: The reasons to take heart are greater than the reasons to lose heart! In other words, we can defeat discouragement because it is only a half-truth. Encouragement does not come from wishful thinking but from seeing the totality of truth and embracing what is truly real.

Let's go back to the story of Elisha and his servant. When they were surrounded by enemies, Elisha said, "Those who are with us are more than those who are with them" (2 Kings 6:16). In the same way, encouragement comes when we are convinced that the reasons to take heart are greater than the reasons to lose heart. When we recognize that these reasons are superior, we can take up the biblical battle cry of hope: "We do not lose heart" (2 Cor. 4:1).

Now I have more bad news. Not only are the reasons to lose heart easy to see but the reasons to take heart are harder to see. Vanquishing discouragement is never automatic nor easy. It is a hard-fought *fight for sight*. But why is it hard? Like Elisha's servant, we are often painfully aware of what is *against* us but woefully unaware of all that is *for* us. Even though the reasons to take heart are greater than the reasons to lose heart, the former can often only be seen "by faith, not by sight" (2 Cor. 5:7).

This is where good news comes back into the picture. The reasons to take heart are actually *more* real than the reasons to lose heart. Now I know that it usually feels the opposite because the things that are physically visible can feel more solid or substantial than the promises of God. But the Bible contradicts that half-truth with this full truth: "The things that are seen are transient, but the things that are unseen are eternal" (2 Cor. 4:18). The things we tangibly see are temporary. The things we cannot see— eternal things—are ultimately more solid and substantial and lasting.

The bottom line in the fight for sight is this: We lose heart when we lose sight of all that we have in Jesus. When we lose sight of Jesus, we see only half the picture, we believe half-truths, and we are robbed of hope. But as believers, we are called to fight back.

> *We lose heart when we lose sight of all that we have in Jesus.*

If we belong to Christ, how can we lose our hope? Christ in us is "the hope of glory" (Col. 1:27). The fallen world we live in has many reasons to lose heart, but Jesus says to you and to me, "Take heart; I have overcome the world" (John 16:33).

Dealing with Discouragement

In this book we will look at the issue of discouragement theologically and practically. The problem with many practical theology books is that they are not always practical or theological. This book aims to be both. In the chapters that follow, we will begin by looking at a big picture of God, and then we will look at how that vision affects the practical details of everyday life. The chapters are short and to the point, because a long book on discouragement would be discouraging.

Part 1 of this book is like an eye exam: Do you see the greatness of God? Do you see all that you have in him? If God is for you, then what could stand against you?

And in part 2, we will dig a little deeper by analyzing some of the real-life reasons that we tend to lose heart. We will examine the past, present, and future problems posed by discouragement and discover biblical reasons to take heart. The conclusion is a stirring reminder of a central theological truth: *God is not done!*

Before We Begin

There are two crucial points of context to understand before beginning to read this book. First, please do not think of discouragement only in individual terms. We are not meant to try to defeat discouragement on our own.

I am convinced that we sometimes read verses like Hebrews 12:1 the wrong way.

> Since we are surrounded by so great a cloud of witnesses, let us also lay aside every weight, and sin which clings so closely, and let us run with endurance the race that is set before us.

What enters into your mind when you read this verse? Too often we picture running a race all by ourselves. It is easy to understand why; no one can run for us. This truth also applies to the Christian life: Each of us must run our own race.

But this way of reading the text misses the full truth: None of us runs alone. You and I share in a massive community of believers called the communion of saints. We can look around at the godly men and women who have finished the race and are now cheering us on and reminding us that God is faithful. We can also turn to our left and our right to see our brothers and sisters in Christ running along beside us.

There is strength in numbers. Do not try to fight discouragement on your own.

I will never forget an inspiring story I read about the Hanna High cross-country team in Anderson, South Carolina.[1] The people in the stands would come to support their children, but they would cheer the loudest for the runner who always finished last.

There is strength in numbers. Do not try to fight discouragement on your own.

That student, Ben Comen, had cerebral palsy. Ben's condition caused him to fall constantly because he did not lift his feet high enough when he ran. He tripped on everything and fell hard because his brain could not send signals fast enough to get his arms underneath him to cushion the fall. After every race, Ben ended up bruised and bloodied, but he never quit. He always finished last, but he always finished.

Grown men would break down and weep while watching this display of perseverance. Ben's teammates would go back out on the course to run the last ten minutes of the race with him. The girls' team would also join, and sometimes runners from opposing teams would go back and run with him as well. They would finish the race together.

That is a great picture of Hebrews 12:1 in action: "Let *us* run with endurance the race that is set before *us*." Most of our "races" will not be like a cross-country challenge. The typical life is more like a Tough Mudder with obstacles all around us (razor wire, mud, freezing water, electric lines) and obstacles within (mental and physical fatigue). Life throws similar challenges at us (unexpected medical bills, extended family drama, loss of a job, etc.). But the race of life doesn't last forever, and the stakes are much, much higher. Do not attempt to fight this battle against discouragement alone. Find the most Bible-believing, grace-soaked, Christ-exalting church you can. Put yourself on the path of grace where you will hear the word of Christ, and link arms with others who will run the race with you. The picture of Hebrews 12 fits with the popular African proverb that says, "If you want to go fast, go alone, but if you want to go far, go together." Let's fight together, run together, and finish together.

Now let me say a word to those of you who are coming to this book with deep wounds. Perhaps you are trying to fight the good fight and run the race with deep-seated trauma, brokenness, or depression (2 Tim. 4:7). Though you desperately try to combat discouragement by filling your mind with biblical truth, you still find that anxiety, panic, and fear constantly threaten to hijack your brain and body in ways that seem to override anything you believe in your heart to be true. If this describes your daily reality, then you may feel as if I'm asking you to run a marathon with a broken leg or climb a flight of stairs in a wheelchair.

The last thing I want is for you to feel condemned because you cannot run the race as fast as someone else. There is no shame in using crutches if you have a broken leg, and wheelchair ramps are a wonderful gift from God. I believe that God has provided good gifts such as medication and God-honoring, clinically informed, gospel-saturated counseling for those who run the race of faith with conditions that seem to make everything harder. As you read the biblical truths in this book, please do not forget the truth that Jesus is our gentle Savior. He would never break or despise a bruised reed (Matt. 12:20).

This book is not a simplistic replacement for the specialized kinds of professional help that address the complexities of pain and trauma and deep darkness. I am not a medical doctor and do not have expertise in counseling people who are clinically depressed or suffer from considerable trauma. However, even if you are walking through deep darkness, this book can still provide crucial, biblical help.

Many Christians will attest that becoming a Christian does not mean that their struggle with depression comes to an end, but it does change some of the dynamics of the struggle. Before coming to Christ, depression can feel like a bottomless pit—a free fall into a dark abyss with no end in sight. After becoming a Christian, depression may still feel like being plunged into darkness, but there is something underneath the darkness—solid ground to stand on.

This book is not designed to treat depression, but my prayer is that it can provide something solid for you to *stand on* when you feel discouraged and struggle in the dark places.[2] This book is a call to take the sword of truth and the shield of faith and *stand against* the sophisticated half-truths of discouragement.

PART ONE

•••

HOW TO FIGHT
FOR SIGHT

PART 1 OF THIS BOOK is like a trip to the optometrist to get our vision tested. Because discouragement is a fight for sight, we are going to look away from counterfeit hopes and fix our gaze on the greatness of the blessed Holy Trinity. Chapter 1 looks at the greatness of God the Father, chapter 2 gazes at the greatness of God the Son, and chapter 3 unveils the greatness of God the Holy Spirit. We are not just asking for a vision from God but a vision of God.

Each chapter will ask us to check something different in our fight for sight. In chapter 1, we will check the scale— not to check our weight but to check our sight. Checking the scale is a call to replace our earthly scale with one that is God-sized. Chapter 2 is a call to check the score. We will look away from counterfeit scoreboards and turn to see the score that matters for all eternity. Chapter 3 is a call to check our story. We all have a sense of how to tell our own story, but is it accurate? Who gets to tell our story? We will see how the God who writes our story also gets to tell our story.

ONE

What to Do When
You Feel Overwhelmed

WHEN I TURNED FOURTEEN, I received a restricted South Dakota driver's permit and I bought my first car—a 1968 Chevrolet Monte Carlo. It had a big engine, which made it easy to speed.

As I drove into my hometown one day, I ignored the speed limit decrease from fifty-five miles per hour to twenty-five. Before I could slow down, a cop clocked me going forty-eight. I had been saving up for a nice car stereo at the time. Instead, all my savings went toward paying that speeding ticket. In addition to draining my funds, I had to borrow money from a family member to cover the rest of the fee. Suddenly I was not only broke but I was also in debt.

One mistake took me from a surplus to a deficit. In the brief time it took the highway patrolman to run my license plate and hand me a slip of paper, I went from encouraged to totally discouraged. I felt like a failure for getting a speeding ticket and losing my meager savings.

The Problem: We Use the Wrong Scale of Measure

On a small scale, this is what often happens to us in life. We look at the various problems that we encounter, and we determine their significance using the wrong scale of measure.

We Count Our Problems

One way we inaccurately measure our problems is by counting them using the wrong equation. The process goes something like this: First, we instinctively try to assess the value of what we want or need. And second, we calculate if we currently have enough to attain those wants and needs. If what we want seems greater than what we have, we often end up getting discouraged.

Here is a simple sketch for the intuitive way we tend to work out this equation in life:

WHAT WE HAVE – WHAT WE NEED = HOW WE FEEL

If what we have is more than what we need, then we feel that the situation is hopeful. However, if what we have is not enough to cover what we want, then our hope takes a major hit. For example, imagine that you received an unexpected and large car repair bill. If you have $250 in your checking account but you are suddenly hit with a $500 bill, your bank balance would be in the negative.

Looking at these circumstances, we might say that your financial security just took a huge hit. It is hard to separate the balance in our bank accounts from the hope in our hearts. Financial hits take a toll on our hope. The greater the hit, the deeper the hole and the darker the despair.

We live in a world that is much more complicated than mere financial analysis. Money is one measurement of the significance of our problems, but it is not the only one. There are many, many more ways to measure the circumstances we face in life. We may measure how meaningful our lives are by calculating if we have enough friends or enough popularity or enough success at work or at school or at parenting or in sports. We may measure our worth based on whether we have the approval of the right person or group.

We Weigh Our Problems

Another way we miscalculate our problems is by weighing them on the wrong scale. We instinctively look at every area of our lives and don't just count our problems but also weigh each of them.

That same summer I got the speeding ticket, my grandpa died of stomach cancer. I did not simply add those problems up in an equation: 1 speeding ticket + 1 death in the family = 2 total problems. Losing my grandpa felt like a much heavier loss than losing my savings.

It was the first time that I had lost somebody I loved. When my grandpa died, I felt as if my world was crashing down around me. Everything seemed to be going wrong. I even wondered why I should go on living.

We can all relate to the weariness of trying to navigate the ups and downs of life. Just when we think everything is going well and the hope in our hearts begins to rise, something happens unexpectedly that knocks us off balance and causes us to lose that hope. We are continually weighing life's assets and liabilities against one another on the scale of hope and despair.

Something happened to me that summer that changed everything. After my grandpa was diagnosed, he told me that it was worth going through stomach cancer if even one of his grandchildren grew closer to God because of it. After he passed away, I realized I was the answer to his dying prayer.

This awareness felt intensely personal, and through this experience, God became very real to me. In the pit of my despair and pain, God began to speak to me in his Word and through sermons and songs. I began to sense God's presence and encouragement as I sought him in worship. The hymns I sang became more like the language and longings of my grieving heart, rather than mere words and notes on a page.

This process of facing heartache and loss helped me see what my perennial problem was. The two major problems I was facing—my financial insecurity and my family loss— felt overwhelmingly big because I could only see half of the story. I was looking only at the negative aspects of my current situation and its effects on my life. My issue was that I had taken God out of the equation.

The Solution: Check the Scale

How did I go from losing heart to taking heart? No, the money did not magically reappear in my checking account. I did not get my grandpa back. But I did check the scale I was using to evaluate my problems. When I opened my eyes to the biggest reality in the universe, God came into the equation in a big way.

Looking back now, I can see how this principle plays out in many different scenarios. When we use the wrong scale of measure and take God out of the equation, we can lose heart. Discouragement is only a half-truth; it sees the truth of a challenging situation, but it lies about God's part in solving the issue. Yes, all the things stacked against us may feel very big, but they do not add up to the full picture.

We lose heart when we buy into the lie that our difficulties are bigger than God.

We lose heart when we buy into the lie that our difficulties are bigger than God, and we lose the fight for sight when we fail to see God correctly. When perception and reality don't align properly, it is easy to become discouraged.

Something similar happens when we look up at the night sky. Most of us have heard the children's song "Twinkle, Twinkle, Little Star." These familiar lyrics are a good example of a situation in which perception and reality are far removed from each other. The stars in the night sky are not little, but they can appear deceptively small because of their massive distance from Earth.

How should we handle this common difficulty between perception and reality? Pastor and author John Piper gives a helpful corrective.

The problem is that in the night sky the wonders of the heavens do not appear as they really are. They seem small and not very bright or awesome. So we must magnify them. That's what a telescope is for. Not to make them look bigger than they are. But to help us, in our weakness, to stop thinking of them as small and show us how great they really are.[1]

He described the example of a comet that passed by the Earth. It was named after a Japanese astronomer named Hyakutake. At its nearest point, Comet Hyakutake was about ten million miles away from Earth. When it passed by our planet, the comet was large enough for people to see it easily, though it appeared smudgy.

Piper went on to explain that even though people could observe the comet with the naked eye, they needed a telescope to get the full picture.

> If you can magnify Hyakutake, and show me that a smudgy softball is really 30,000 miles across (four times the size of the earth), I will be more amazed. Or if you can magnify the tail and show me that a dim cloudy trail of light a few handbreadths in width is really 6,000,000 miles long, then I will feel differently about this amazing thing called a comet.[2]

In the same way, we need to stop thinking of God as small. Our hearts are easy prey when God seems small, because our problems seem bigger than God can handle. But as a telescope reveals the true size of the stars, Scripture gives us an accurate scale to use to resize our problems in light of the greatness of God.

To reset the scales, we must begin by repenting of our false assessment and false measures. Repenting involves replacing and then resizing. We start by replacing our human-centered measurements with God-centered ones. Doing that allows us to resize the situation in light of God's greatness. Instead of saying prayers that turn into a gripe session in which we tell God how big our problems are, we can begin to battle discouragement when we tell our hearts (and our problems) how big our God is.

We can begin to battle discouragement when we tell our hearts (and our problems) how big our God is.

How to Gain a Proper Perspective

It is important to put our problems into proper perspective. I am not saying that the things that we are facing are small because our problems are often big and overwhelming and beyond our ability to handle. We do not need to minimize how big or painful our problems are, but they can only become small when we view them in comparison to the greatness of God.

Isaiah 40 gives us a helpful example of this point. God's people were discouraged because they seemed so weak in comparison to the powerful nation that held them in captivity. The problem was that the Israelites were believing a half-truth. Yes, their captors were stronger—the Babylonians were not a small problem!—but the Israelites were using the wrong scale to evaluate the issue. They had removed God from the equation and were comparing themselves to their captors instead of comparing their captors to their Savior.

In response to their distress, God comforted his people by confronting them and calling them to check their scales again. I could spend the rest of this book expounding the images of Isaiah 40, but I will limit myself to two examples in which God says, "Who has measured the waters in the hollow of his hand . . . and weighed the mountains in scales?" (v. 12).

Measure the Waters

The first image focuses on God's ability to measure "the waters in the hollow of his hand."

One day I tried to meditate on this image by using myself as an example. I wondered, *How much water* can *I measure in the hollow of my hand?* I grabbed a measuring cup, filled it, and then tried to pour a full cup of water into the hollow of my cupped hand. It makes me laugh now to think about how much I overestimated the size of my hand. I made a total mess on the counter when I tried to pour that cup of water into my hand. I learned my lesson and did all my subsequent tests over the sink.

Next, I tried half a cup of water. Not even close. I went down to a tablespoon of water. Still too much. I humbled myself further and grabbed a measuring teaspoon. Finally, the water stayed put (though a few drops slipped out). I can *almost* hold a teaspoon of water in the hollow of my hand. Needless to say, I felt very small.

The contrast between God's capabilities and my own hit home in a fresh way. How much water can God hold in the hollow of his hand? Isaiah does not reach for a measuring cup, and he does not provide us with any limits or percentages of how much water God can hold. He just says that God held "the waters"—meaning all of them. How much water is that? The best estimate we can make is that the Earth has about 332.5 million cubic miles of water. A cubic mile of water equals more than 1.1 trillion gallons.[3]

God is off-the-charts, out-of-this-world greater than we can fathom.

That number can make your head spin. While we are busy trying to multiply 1.1 trillion gallons by 332.5 million, God simply says, "Here, let me use myself as the standard of measure. All the waters from all the ponds, lakes, rivers, and oceans on planet Earth fill only a small space in my hand."

Those who cannot hold a teaspoon of water should trust in the One who cups the oceans in the hollow of his hand like a few drops from a faucet. God is off-the-charts, out-of-this-world greater than we can fathom.

Weigh the Mountains

The second image of the Father's greatness involves picking something up and weighing it on a scale. "Who has . . . weighed the mountains in scales?"

Weighing things on scales is a familiar experience for most of us. Have you ever picked up a bunch of bananas at the grocery store and then put them on a scale to see how much they weighed? Now change that image and make it God-sized. We weigh bananas; God weighs the mountains.

How can we even begin to estimate how much all the mountains on Earth weigh? We struggle to find an accurate measurement for even one mountain. Take Mount Everest as an example. If we start with the height of 11,500 feet from Base Camp to summit, then we can estimate that the volume of Mount Everest is around 2.1 trillion cubic feet. Multiply that by the density, and Everest tips the scale at about 357 trillion pounds.[4] However, that number is still an approximate weight because it doesn't include the weight of the snow and ice.

How much is 357 trillion pounds? We couldn't find a crane big enough to lift it, and there is no scale in the world strong enough to weigh it. But the weight of the mountains is nothing to God. He could pick them all up in one hand and skip them like stones across the oceans. The oceans, remember, that he holds in the hollow of his other hand.

God is the standard of measure for everything we encounter or experience in our lives.

The psalmist says of God, "His greatness is unsearchable" (Ps. 145:3). When we are confronted with the truth of that statement, we struggle to comprehend such greatness. There is no scale that could measure it. It would be like trying to weigh a blue whale on a bathroom scale. Our scale will break every time.

The greatness of the Father cannot be measured on a scale because he *is* the scale. God is the standard of measure for everything we encounter or experience in our lives.

Apply the Scale

How do these God-sized images help us take heart when we feel discouraged? After I preached on Isaiah 40 one weekend, I heard that the reality of God's greatness described in that passage became a lifeline for a couple that was visiting our church on a very difficult weekend. They were in town because their child needed a major surgery. The situation was panic-inducing and heart-wrenching, and they felt crushed by the weight of their concerns. In effect, they were using their own scale of how much weight they could bear, and the situation was far too heavy.

Then the truth of God's greatness landed on them in fresh ways through the words of Isaiah 40. They stopped weighing their issues using their human abilities and started relying on the power of God as their standard. From that point on, whenever they would start to worry, one of them would put out their hand and cup it as if measuring water. This symbol served as a stirring reminder of the greatness of the God who holds all the waters of the world in the hollow of his hand. That image instantly resized the situation for them. When the weight of their situation started to bury them in discouragement, faith would rise again with the reminder of God's greatness.

There are two lies in particular that seem to plague God's people and create a scourge of discouragement. We become easy targets for despair when God seems small or when he seems absent.

When God Seems Small

All too often, we do the exact opposite of Isaiah 40. We take small things and blow them out of proportion so that they become bigger than God. The audacity of our idolatry is that we think our problems are too big for God to handle.

When I was growing up, I watched the popular movies *Honey, I Shrunk the Kids* and *Honey, I Blew Up the Kid*.

Discouragement grows when we shrink God down to our size.

In both of those films, hilarity ensues when things are blown out of proportion—either too small or too big. In the movies, making things too large or too small results in lighthearted comedy, but resizing when it comes to our problems is a tragedy. We take the greatness of God and shrink him down to our size, while at the same time blowing up and magnifying our problems to be greater than God. It should shake us to the core to see how easily and how frequently we repeat that process.

Discouragement grows when we shrink God down to our size.

When God Seems Absent

The fact that God sometimes seems small is not the only problem we face. Sometimes God seems far away or far removed from our lives. We desperately search for God's presence in our lives, but we can't seem to find him. He feels distant or even absent. At those times, the issue is not only that we doubt God's power but also that we doubt his presence. We wonder if he has forsaken us.

A close friend of mine had to face the heart-wrenching realities of cancer. The chemotherapy, the hair loss, the nausea, the fatigue, the uncertainty of life expectancy, the medical bills, and the constant pain all took a toll on his fight for hope, but he said the single hardest struggle of all was walking through these things with an aching sense of God's absence at times. The feeling that God was not there for him in his struggles, he told me, was far worse than all the other burdens combined.

God gets right to the point in addressing that lie in the book of Isaiah. Many of us have struggled with exactly the same complaint that Isaiah's readers expressed in chapter 49. They heard that God was powerful and wise, but they doubted his presence. They felt abandoned, so they cried out in anguish, "The LORD has forsaken me; my Lord has forgotten me" (Isa. 49:14).

God declares that his love is unconditional.

In response, God compares himself to a mother. He said to his people, "Can a woman forget her nursing child, that she should have no compassion on the son of her womb? Even these may forget, *yet I will not forget you*" (Isa. 49:15).

Good mothers are fiercely protective of their children, but because all humans are flawed, there are some sad exceptions to this general principle. Maternal love is not a guarantee in this life. However, God declares that his love is unconditional and he will never leave us nor forsake us (Deut. 31:6).

Engraved on God's Hands

In Isaiah, God continued to assure the despairing people of Israel of his presence with this beautiful word picture: "Behold, I have engraved you on the palms of my hands" (49:16).

It was fairly common in the ancient world for a master's name to be tattooed on his servant. In an earlier chapter, Isaiah referred to this practice when he testified that some people have the name of the Lord written on their hand: "This one will say, 'I am the LORD's,' another will call on the name of Jacob, and another will write on his hand, 'The LORD's'" (Isa. 44:5).

But it is with this point that the power of the gospel blows away all our expectations. Never in the ancient world would one see the name of a servant tattooed on their master—ever. That would put the master in the role of the servant, and who could imagine a master devoting his life to serve?

Christians can imagine a master like this, because the High King of heaven became a servant to save his people.

The words of Isaiah 49:16 convey the principle of God's love for his people. In the New Testament, the gospel literally put flesh on that principle. Jesus Christ, the Son of God, came as a servant and said that he "came not to be served but to serve, and to give his life as a ransom for many" (Mark 10:45).

The miracle of God coming to earth as a baby is mind-blowing. The God who heaven and earth cannot contain—the same God who measures the waters in his hand and weighs the mountains in scales—was born as a baby. The perfect, limitless nature and character of God are perfectly revealed and expressed in the person of Jesus. Not only are all the perfections of God present in Jesus but all the perfections are perfectly joined and perfectly balanced together in a union that is fully God and fully man. Jesus is the image of the invisible God—meaning that he is the invisible God made visible. The writer of the book of Hebrews says Jesus is the "radiance of the glory of God and the exact imprint of his nature" (Heb. 1:3).

Paul unpacks this mind-blowing thought for us in Colossians 2:9: "For in him [Jesus] the whole fullness of deity dwells bodily." This is a one-sentence summary of full orthodoxy on the natures of Christ. He is truly God ("whole fullness of deity"), and he is truly man ("dwells bodily"). Jesus is not part God—he is the very nature of God. He is not part man, merely appearing to be human—he is fully human, flesh and blood. Jesus got tired, hungry, and thirsty. He cried and he died. The Bible says he "in every respect has been tempted as we are, yet without sin" (Heb. 4:15).

Is your mind spinning right now? Heaven and earth cannot contain God—yet the whole fullness of deity dwelled in the human body of Jesus Christ.

Isaiah 40:12 asks us to imagine 332.5 million cubic miles of water fitting into the hollow of God's hand. But Colossians 2:9 asks us to imagine something even more awe-inspiring. Imagine something like 332.5 million cubic miles of water—all the oceans of the world without a single drop missing—fitting into a Styrofoam coffee cup. In Jesus Christ, the infinite fullness of deity dwells in a human body with these two natures joined perfectly and indivisibly with nothing missing.

The incarnation takes us right to the brink of what our language can say and our minds can understand, and then it gloriously goes further. Our minds are left defeated, and we confess to God, "You are in another category altogether!"

The Son of God was forsaken on the cross so that we will never be.

Adore the wisdom. Celebrate the mystery. Thank God for the incarnation of Jesus. He came to be a servant, and he gave himself as a sacrifice for our sins. The sacrifice of his Son shows God's incredible love for the world. It is not too good to be true. He really came. He really suffered. He really died. The Son of God was forsaken on the cross so that we will never be.

You may be facing problems that seem overwhelming right now. If you begin to lose sight of God's presence in the midst of your struggles, remember this: Your Father has not forsaken you. He will never leave you or forsake you. We have this promise not only in writing but in blood.

Not a Tame Theology

Don't buy the lie of discouragement. Your situation is not bigger than God's ability to handle it. Whenever you are tempted to give in to despair, cup your hands together. Be comforted as you are confronted with the greatness of God. Don't forget that God won't forget you. Hope again.

One way to cultivate hope is to memorize and meditate on passages of Scripture that confront our small views of God with glimpses of his greatness. Here are just a few of the many verses that highlight the greatness of God.

> It is he who sits above the circle of the earth,
> and its inhabitants are like grasshoppers. (Isa. 40:22)

Will God indeed dwell on the earth? Behold, heaven and the highest heaven cannot contain you. (1 Kings 8:27)

> Great is the LORD, and greatly to be praised,
>   and his greatness is unsearchable. (Ps. 145:3)

Ah, Lord GOD! It is you who have made the heavens and the earth by your great power and by your outstretched arm! Nothing is too hard for you. (Jer. 32:17)

These are not tame truths. No matter what your circumstances might be right now, don't lose sight of God. Don't shrink him down to a human-sized scale. Fight off the cold chill of discouragement by fanning these truths into flames. Prayerfully look upon the big truths of God until you can proclaim along with the hymnist that "the things of earth . . . grow strangely dim in the light of his glory and grace."[5] We cannot put the Almighty God on a scale or measure his infinite greatness.

Discouragement comes when we domesticate God. Discouragement is defeated when we stop trying to tame God and instead confess with Job:

> I know that you can do all things,
>   and that no purpose of yours can be
>   thwarted. . . .
> Therefore I have uttered what I did not
>   understand,
>   things too wonderful for me, which I did not
>   know. (Job 42:2–3)

In response, we receive gospel hope for our discouraged hearts through the unwavering promise of God, who assures us:

> I have loved you with an everlasting love;
>> therefore I have continued my faithfulness to
>>> you. (Jer. 31:3)

Have the crushing circumstances of life broken your scale? Broken scales lead to broken hearts. I urge you to replace your scale with the God-sized scale of Scripture. By faith, let us take heart as we press on to know the Lord and reset our scales in terms of the greatness of his power, love, and faithfulness.

TWO

What to Do When
You Feel Defeated

MY LAST HIGH SCHOOL basketball game is a memory that
is forever etched in my mind. One scene really stands out.
It was the fourth quarter, our team was playing defense, and
the opposing team dribbled the ball to half court. Suddenly
one of my teammates stole the ball and passed it to me. I
had only one guy to beat to our basket. I outran him and
scored my one and only career slam dunk.

Our fans went wild! I felt as if I was walking on air for a
moment. It was one of the greatest feelings in the world.

But I was in for a rude awakening. The fans from the
opposing team quickly started a chant that shut down our
cheering section: "Check the score, check the score, check
the score!"

Their trash talk hit home. Despite my successful slam dunk, our team was still behind by sixteen points. For a brief moment it felt like we were winning, but our opponents' trash talk quickly brought us back to reality. We were losing, badly.

The Problem: We Forget the Score

In the Christian life, we face many things that make us feel as if we, too, are losing. Christians are being persecuted all over the world. It seems as if we are outmatched and overpowered. Satan's time is short, so he puts a full-court press on us. Oftentimes it feels as if the enemy is winning as he performs showstopping and demoralizing slam dunks. It can look like the church is losing, especially when so many Christians are losing their lives every day.

The same dynamic can happen with our health issues. The Bible says that our physical bodies are "wasting away" (2 Cor. 4:16). When our health or the health of our loved ones takes a hit, it feels like losing. This dynamic becomes even more pressing when the bad news is so severe that we fear the loss of life itself.

This fear also applies to our personal lives. We begin to feel as if we are losing when we become painfully aware of all the ways we are struggling against sin and temptation. We don't even live up to our own standards, let alone God's standards! It feels like we are losing the battle against sin, and it's not long before we start to wonder if God also looks at us as moral losers.

We lose heart when we fail to check the real score because we have forgotten that Christ has already won. The apostle John informs us, "Weep no more; behold, the Lion of the tribe of Judah, the Root of David, has conquered" (Rev. 5:5). The victory is not in question.

We lose heart when we fail to check the real score.

Don't take Jesus out of the equation! We memorize verses such as Jesus's final words on the cross: "It is finished" (John 19:30). Or his promise to us: "Take heart; I have overcome the world" (John 16:33). We know these verses, but do we live in the light of them? The fact that Christ will never die again and that death has no dominion over him is a game changer. There is never a reason for us to renew the challenge in order to see who will win.

Every year, people fill out brackets for NCAA basketball's March Madness. Every year the process has to be repeated. The various college teams compete to see which one will win each season. No one ever tries to renew the challenge by going back to beat the 1966–67 UCLA Bruins. They won, and that is a fact. That season is finished.

When Jesus defeated death, he broke the bracket. It is finished. Now the only question is whether we will partake in his victory or suffer destruction and defeat with his enemies.

We Know the Future

The fact that Christ has defeated death also means that we know the future. Let that sink in.

When I was a kid, I watched the movie *Back to the Future II*. The villain of the movie, Biff—what a great name for a villain!—travels to the future and finds a sports almanac. He becomes very wealthy because he can place winning bets on every game because he knows every outcome. As a kid, I can remember thinking how awesome it would be to have an almanac like that. If I had an almanac that recorded future events, I would be a major moron if I started

I know how the game ends. I know the eternal score. We win.

sweating bullets when a game came down to the wire. I would already know the winner, so there would be no need to stress.

After I became a believer, I saw the movie again. But as I rewatched the film, I saw it through a different set of eyes. As a kid, I thought it would be great to have Biff's sports almanac. Then it dawned on me. As a believer, I have a far better almanac than the one in the movie. Why am I so anxious and worried about so many things? I know how the game ends. I know the eternal score. We win.

Apply the Score

Are you using a scoreboard in your life to keep track of successes versus failures? Are you consistently calculating your perceived wins versus losses, achievements versus setbacks, and compliments versus criticisms? If so, you are checking the wrong scoreboard. It is easy to do, but it is liberating to check the real score.

What does it mean to check the score when we are faced with the half-truths of persecution, personal sin, or health problems? Let's take a look at each of these sophisticated lies below and apply the score so that we can take heart and defeat discouragement.

The Half-Truth of Persecution

First, don't believe the half-truth of persecution. Yes, Satan is persecuting the church. That is undeniable. Some researchers estimate that as many as one hundred thousand Christians are martyred every year.[1] These numbers make it look like the church is losing. But check the score. Satan is persecuting Christians so frantically because he knows he will lose, not because he thinks he has a chance of winning. He knows his time is short. Satan and his demons have checked the final score—

Satan is persecuting Christians so frantically because he knows he will lose, not because he thinks he has a chance of winning.

the Bible has a record of how that conversation went. When the demons encountered Jesus on Earth, they asked him if he had come to destroy them "before the time" (Matt 8:29). Their time is coming, their doom is imminent, and they know it.

In the final book of the Bible, we get a sneak peek of the devil's destruction. The apostle John wrote, "The devil who had deceived them was thrown into the lake of fire and sulfur where the beast and the false prophet were, and they will be tormented day and night forever and ever" (Rev. 20:10).

The Half-Truth of Personal Sin

Second, don't let the half-truth of personal sin cause you to lose sight of the score. Do you feel as if you are losing your faith battle because you see your sin so clearly? Check the score! The debt of your sin has been canceled and nailed to the cross with Christ: "God made [us] alive together with him, having forgiven us all our trespasses, by canceling the record of debt that stood against us with its legal demands. This he set aside, nailing it to the cross" (Col. 2:13–14).

Check the score. You bear your sins no more. God has removed it from you "as far as the east is from the west" (Ps. 103:12). Do you see the greatness of God in the cross of Jesus Christ?

Take a moment to contemplate the distance involved in the image of removing sin as far as the east is from the west. Pastor Sam Storms once shared a devotional message that made this word picture come alive for me.

The Hubble Telescope has given us breathtaking pictures of a galaxy some 13 billion light years from earth. Remember that a light year is 6,000,000,000,000 (six trillion) miles. That put this galaxy at 78,000,000,000,000,000,000,000 miles from earth! In case you were wondering, we count from million, to billion, to quadrillion, to quintillion, to sextillion. So, this galaxy is 78 sextillion miles from earth.

If you traveled 500 mph non-stop, literally 60 minutes of every hour, 24 hours in every day, seven days in every week, 52 weeks in every year, with not a moment's pause or delay, it would take you 20,000,000,000,000,000 years (that's 20 quadrillion years) to get there! And that would only get you to the farthest point that our best telescopes have yet been able to detect. Still, this would be the mere fringe of what lies beyond.

My point—and the point of the psalmist—is that the magnitude of such a distance is a pathetically small comparison to the likelihood that you will ever be dealt with according to your sin or repaid for your iniquities! If you were ever inclined to pursue your transgressions so that you might place yourself beneath their condemning power, 78,000,000,000,000,000,000,000 miles is an infinitesimally small fraction of the distance you must travel to find them![2]

If you struggle with a chronic sense of guilt and shame, then check the score: You bear your sins no more. If your sin seems to stick close to you, check again. Sometimes we can look at the side mirror of a car and a message warns us, "Objects in the mirror are closer than they appear." Our sin is similar; it seems closer to us than it is. But remember, God has removed it as far as the east is from the west.

The Half-Truth of Health Problems

Third, do not let the half-truth of health problems keep you from checking the score. Is your health deteriorating? Have you received a scary diagnosis like cancer that feels as if it defines your life? Check the score! The resurrection is the great game changer. Death is not defeat, because Christ defeated death.

Add your voice to the apostle Paul's in trash talking the opponent: "O death, where is your victory? O death, where is your sting?" (1 Cor. 15:55), and join the crowd of believers as together we chant the victory of our faith: "Christ is risen from the dead. Check the score, check the score, he's alive forevermore!"

Death is not defeat, because Christ defeated death.

Does the struggle for hope in the midst of health problems still seem theoretical and abstract? This next story will make it a little more concrete and personal.

No Less Saved

Martyn Lloyd-Jones was perhaps the greatest preacher of his generation. Toward the end of his life, Martyn became feeble and sick, and it took this renowned theologian a very long time to get from his chair to his bed. Friends would come to encourage him, but as they watched him struggle physically, they would become discouraged themselves. His friends would wonder how he could face these trials and maintain such a thankful heart. They'd wonder if Martyn was discouraged now that he could no longer be active and preach like before.

In response, Martyn would often quote Luke 10:20: "Nevertheless, do not rejoice in this, that the spirits are subject to you, but rejoice that your names are written in heaven." He would also add his own words, "Our relationship to

God is to be the supreme cause of joy." In fact, he would point out that he was not discouraged because salvation was nearer to him at that point than when he first believed.[3]

Your future victory is so certain that you can rejoice in it now.

What about you? Are you struggling with the loss of a job, the loss of health, or the loss of a relationship? Here is the question: "Why should you be discouraged? Are you any less saved today than you were the moment you came to faith in Christ?" The Bible says your name is written in heaven. Don't lose sight of all that Christ purchased for you. Your future victory is so certain that you can rejoice in it now.

THREE

What to Do When
You Feel Worthless

ONE TUESDAY MORNING, a young woman came into my office for counseling. Wiping away her tears, she confessed, "I am struggling in my relationship with God."

I nodded in empathy and encouragement. Then I asked her, "Why do you think it is such a struggle?"

She responded, "I just feel like God is irritated and frustrated with me. I have deep doubts that God even loves me."

"How has God made it clear to you that he feels such frustration toward you?" I asked.

There was an awkward pause for a moment as she struggled to answer. After what felt like a long time, she finally ended up saying, "Well, God did not make it clear to me. It is just the way that I feel."

"Ah, I see. Tell me a little more about how you feel about you."

She took a deep breath and looked at the floor of my office. "I am having such a hard time forgiving myself. I confess my sin and receive forgiveness, but then I fall into the same sin patterns again."

Gently, I asked her, "Do you think you might be lumping together what God feels about you with how you feel about you?"

The Problem: We Project Our Feelings onto God

This young woman was not alone in her struggle to believe that God really loved her. I have seen multiple versions of this story play out over the years in my pastoral counseling.

This process is called projection. People assume that God is deeply disappointed or frustrated *with them* because they are deeply disappointed or frustrated *with themselves*. It is important for us to check our assumptions instead of projecting them.

Discouragement is like a pair of sunglasses that makes all of life seem darker. When we are discouraged, we often take our unflattering personal reflections and transfer those dark thoughts and feelings to God. We make the faulty assumption that "God must look at me the way I look at me."

Take a moment and examine your self-talk or your inner dialogue. What kinds of things do you say to yourself on a regular basis? Consider whether your self-talk includes negative statements, such as "I'm not smart enough." "I'm not strong enough." "I'm just going to fail anyway." "Why try? I'll never be able to do this." "I'm a loser." "No one will ever love me."

I am still shocked by my own self-talk. I speak very harshly to myself, saying things that I would never say to anyone else.

We need to lay down the weapons that we aim at ourselves and check our stories against God's story.

The Solution: Check the Story

We can either project onto God what we think about ourselves or we can receive from God what he says about us. Revelation is the opposite of projection. The process looks something like this:

REVELATION	PROJECTION
GOD	GOD
↓	↑
US	US

The opposite of projecting what we think about ourselves *onto God* is receiving what he says about us *from God*.

We will get our stories wrong and become discouraged every time unless we let God be the narrator.

Where do we go to check our misguided beliefs and hear God's version? The full story can be found in God's Word.

We will get our stories wrong and become discouraged every time unless we let God be the narrator.

Let's pause for a moment and think through why it can be so spiritually stirring and life-giving to read what God says in his Word. What does it mean when we say the Bible is God's Word? The apostle Paul provides what is perhaps the clearest answer to this question. In 2 Timothy 3:16, Paul says, "All Scripture is breathed out by God." Many Scripture versions translate the word for *breathed out* in the Greek text as *inspired*, but it actually means *expired*—not as in having reached its expiration date but as in physically breathing out.

This description offers a profoundly powerful picture of what the Bible is; it is the very breath of God.

This process is similar to the way God created Adam. The Bible says that on the sixth day, God formed Adam from the dust of the ground and "breathed into his nostrils the breath of life, and the man became a living creature" (Gen. 2:7). In the Garden of Eden, God breathed out the breath of life, and that breath went into the dust and the man became alive.

As with Adam, God breathed life into the Bible (2 Tim. 3:16). How can we receive God's life-giving breath today? We open God's Word and breathe it in.

The Story of Your Salvation

The breathed-out words of the Bible tell us the true story of how God made us alive. Yet there are many counterfeit versions of our story that we can tell ourselves.

For example, I sometimes hear people bemoan that their testimony is boring. They say that they were raised in a Christian home and are not quite sure when they got saved. They were nurtured in the truth of the gospel from an early age and have not openly rebelled in a lawless kind of way. Prior to coming to Christ, they were never arrested for a crime, they were never addicted to drugs, and they never slept around. Therefore they think their testimony of coming to faith in Jesus is boring because they never lived a wild and reckless life.

Perhaps your testimony is something like that. If so, you may have avoided a list of notorious sins, but that doesn't mean that your salvation is boring. You have believed a half-truth. People who think that salvation is boring do not really know their story. Everything changes when we allow God to tell our story. Look at the way he shares it in his Word.

> *But God*, being rich in mercy, because of the great love with which he loved us, even when we were dead in our trespasses, made us alive together with Christ—by grace you have been saved—and raised us up with him and seated us with him in the heavenly places in Christ Jesus. (Eph. 2:4–6)

In God's version of the story, no one has a boring testimony for one simple reason: Being raised from the dead is *not* boring. You may feel like a mess or a failure, but that is only a half-truth. The full story shows that you are a God-wrought miracle.

Don't water down the beauty of salvation. It is not as if you were on the brink of drowning and then God threw a life preserver with SALVATION printed in red letters within your reach so that, if you would just grab it, he could pull you in. Not at all!

You are not boring; you are not a mess; you are a miracle!

In God's version of the story, you were "dead" (Eph. 2:5). You were not drowning and *almost* dead; you had already drowned and were stone-cold dead at the bottom of the lake as a child of wrath. God had to *make* you alive. He dove to the bottom of the lake, pulled your dead body up to the shore, breathed the breath of life into you—performing the miracle of divine mouth-to-mouth resuscitation—and "made [you] alive" (Eph. 2:5). Salvation is not merely the *offer* of life but the *giving* of life.

Christianity is not about bad people becoming better; it is about dead people becoming alive. You are not boring; you are not a mess; you are a miracle!

Why did God save us and give us new life? This text answers that question with bold clarity that heralds God's heart: "Because of the great love with which he loved us" (Eph. 2:4). God did not love us because we were lovely. He loved us because God is love and he chose us as his children.

You are alive because God first loved you.

The same dynamic of our salvation being a result of God's love appears in Deuteronomy 7:7–8.

> It was not because you were more in number than any other people that *the LORD set his love on you and chose you*, for you were the fewest of all peoples, but it is *because the LORD loves you* and is keeping the oath that he swore to your fathers, that the LORD has brought you out with a mighty hand and redeemed you from the house of slavery, from the hand of Pharaoh king of Egypt.

He set his love on you because he loves you! Are you trying to make yourself perfect to earn his love? If so, you are living the wrong story. The true story says that you are alive because God first loved you.

The Story of God's Love

The reason that God's unconditional love is so hard to grasp is that human love operates on such a different wavelength. Human love is a reaction of attraction. It starts with a person's loveliness, which leads to the response of love. In other words, human love sets its love on that which is already lovely.

The divine love of the Father is gloriously different. God does not look around to find the best people to love because they are already good. God's perfectly pure eyes would not find any moral loveliness among the mass of sinful humanity. But do not fall into the trap of thinking that God the Father is the angry member of the Trinity and Jesus is the loving one who has to keep the Father in check.

Try this theological quiz on for size. I will make two statements, and you will determine whether they are true.

1. "God loves us because Christ died for us."

That statement can be misleading because it does not factor in the Father's love that led him to send the Son. John 3:16 declares, "God so loved the world, that *he* gave his only Son, that whoever believes in him should not perish but have eternal life." Without the love of God the Father, there would be no sending of the Son to save us from our own shortcomings.

When we factor in the love of the Father, we can then affirm the truth of the second statement.

2. "*Because* God loves us, Christ died for us."

God loved us before he sent his Son to earth. The love of the Father came before the cross of Christ. And it was his love for us that led him to send his Son to die for us so that we could be reunited one day.

We see the love of God in sending his Son to save us from our sinfulness so that we could become his children. We can say with the apostle John, "See what kind of love the Father has given to us, that we should be called children of God; and so we are" (1 John 3:1).

The Holy Spirit Spotlights the Story

Whenever we are tempted to become discouraged, we should check to make sure we have our stories straight. In Christ, we are children of God. As children of God, we are the objects of God's love—not because of anything we have done but because he chose to love us. This is our story.

We are the objects of God's love—not because of anything we have done but because he chose to love us. This is our story.

The Holy Spirit brings the story of God's love home to our hearts. How? The Holy Spirit does not draw attention to himself. He has been called the shy member of the Trinity because the Spirit does not reveal himself; he reveals Christ.

I love how J. I. Packer makes this point in *Keep in Step with the Spirit*.

> I remember walking to a church one winter evening to preach on the words, "he shall glorify me," seeing the building floodlit as I turned a corner, and realizing that this was exactly the illustration my message needed. When floodlighting is well done, the floodlights are so placed that you do not see them; you are not in fact supposed to see where the light is coming from; what you are meant to see is just the building on which the floodlights are trained. The intended effect is to make it visible when otherwise it would not be seen for the darkness, and to maximize its dignity by throwing all its details into relief so that you can see it properly. This perfectly illustrates the Spirit's new covenant role. He is, so to speak, the hidden floodlight shining on the Savior.
>
> Or think of it this way. It is as if the Spirit stands behind us, throwing light over our shoulder, on Jesus, who stands facing us. The Spirit's message to us is never, "Look at me; listen to me; come to me; get to know me," but always, "Look at *him*, and see his glory; listen to *him*, and hear his word; go to *him*, and have his life; get to know *him*, and taste his gift of joy and peace."[1]

The Holy Spirit shows us Jesus Christ, who is the way and the truth and the life. No one comes to the Father except through him (John 14:6). He reveals the Father to us so clearly that if we have seen Jesus, we have seen the Father (John 14:9). And Jesus gives us the right to become children of God (1 John 3:1).

The Holy Spirit is profoundly active in making sure that this message of God's love penetrates our defenses. To shine a spotlight on this story, God gives us a double testimony: an external (objective) testimony and an internal (subjective) one.

The External Testimony of the Spirit

God has provided an external testimony of his love through the Bible. The Holy Spirit is the author of Scripture. Peter explains the process of writing the Bible this way: "No prophecy was ever produced by the will of man, but men spoke from God as they were carried along by the Holy Spirit" (2 Pet. 1:21). Scripture is God's personal revelation of his love for us.

Perhaps you struggle to feel the *fact* of God's love. Does your lack of feeling make God's love any less real? The Bible points us to the external testimony of God's love found in the cross of Christ. Romans 5:8 says, "God shows his love for us in that while we were still sinners, Christ died for us."

Remember, God did not love you and me because we were lovely. He loved us while we were still sinners—morally unlovely. Whenever you feel the talons of discouragement sinking into your heart, look to the cross and see the unchanging, unshakable, irreversible love of God as Jesus bore the burden of sin for you and suffered in your place. He was condemned so that you could be accepted. In Christ, the banner flying high over you says "no condemnation" (Rom. 8:1).

The Internal Testimony of the Spirit

God has also provided an internal testimony of his love through the Holy Spirit. Look at the connection between God's love, the Holy Spirit, and the hope in our hearts.

> *Hope* does not put us to shame, because *God's love* has been poured into *our hearts* through *the Holy Spirit* who has been given to us. (Rom. 5:5)

On the one hand, God's love transcends our *subjective* doubts through the objective testimony that exists outside of us at the cross (Rom. 5:8). On the other hand, God's love transcends cerebral calculation because God pours his love into our very hearts through his Holy Spirit (Rom. 5:5).

The Holy Spirit is called "the Spirit of adoption" (Rom. 8:15). The Spirit testifies with our spirits that we are the children of God, causing us to cry out, "Father!"

There are orphanages throughout the world where it is common for babies and young children to be silent. Why? The children have learned that they could cry but no one would answer, so they learned to stop reaching out. Andy Bilson, a British professor of social work, writes, "Without doubt, the most gut wrenching sound I've ever heard is that of silence in a ward full of children in an orphanage. In orphanages throughout Europe, Africa, Asia and South America, babies have learnt not to cry because they realised no one will comfort them. They're ignored. Forgotten. Silent."[2]

In contrast, Christians can cry out because we know we have a Father who will answer. Paul describes our response to God's love in Romans 8:15–16.

> For you did not receive the spirit of slavery to fall back into fear, but you have received the Spirit of adoption as sons, by whom we cry, "Abba! Father!" The Spirit himself bears witness with our spirit that we are children of God.

The Spirit of God is the Spirit of adoption. He testifies to our adoption into the family of God. In his classic book *Knowing God*, J. I. Packer observed that we don't prize the doctrine of being adopted into God's family as we should because it is usually lumped together with justification or the forgiveness of sins. Packer says that adoption is "*the highest privilege that the gospel offers*; higher even than justification."[3]

So how do we avoid lumping justification and adoption together? Justification means that even though we are guilty sinners, we can receive the verdict of "not guilty" on the basis of what Christ has done for us. Christ's life provided the righteousness we need, and Christ's death paid the penalty for our sins. Adoption is an over and above gift of belonging we receive through justification by faith.

Justification says, "You are not guilty." Adoption says, "You are family."

Justification says, "You can go free now." Adoption says, "You can live here always."

People who think of God only as a judge have a hard time feeling the full weight of the glory of salvation, because it is hard to imagine having a deep relationship with a judge. But he is no longer only our judge; he is our loving Father as well! There is a kind of love on display here that should feel lavish and unique.

Through the miracle of adoption, we go through a mind-blowing transformation. Those who were children of wrath are now children of God. The apostle John writes with such a sense of wonder and worship that it seems like he almost falls out of his chair while writing this: "See what kind of love the Father has given to us, that we should be called children of God; and so we are" (1 John 3:1).

We are the children of God. That is our story! Can you believe it?

Hope for the Unreached Places in Your Heart

As we saw earlier, we often think that God is frustrated with us because we are frustrated with ourselves. Deep down, we think that God merely tolerates us. We think, "How could he really and truly love us?"

This is where we need to hear the truth of God's Word herald his heart for his children rather than listen to the lies and half-truths of our discouraged hearts. One of the most stunning promises in the Bible is that God will never stop loving his children. God's *I will* leads to a *that they*.

> *We are the children of God. That is our story! Can you believe it?*

I will give them one heart and one way, *that they* may fear me forever, for their own good and the good of their children after them. *I will* make with them an everlasting covenant, that *I will not* turn away from doing good to them. And *I will* put the fear of me in their hearts, *that they* may not turn from me. *I will* rejoice in doing them good, and *I will* plant them in this land in faithfulness, with all my heart and all my soul. (Jer. 32:39–41)

Show me a chapter and verse in God's Word that says his love for his children is half-hearted! Look again at what God explicitly says. He loves you and rejoices in doing good for you "with all [his] heart and all [his] soul" (Jer. 32:41). This seems too good to be true. Have you ever seen someone do something with every ounce of passion and emotion they could muster? No one ever sees that kind of passion and says, "I wonder if their heart is in it." Imagine what someone could do with an infinite, unlimited heart and unlimited soul!

We won't get to heaven because *we love God* with all of our hearts and souls. We will make it to heaven because *God loves us* with all of his heart and soul. Do you understand that deeply and viscerally? There are places in our hearts where discouragement has permanently dispossessed hope, but the love of God gives us a mission of hope in our hearts. We all know that there are unreached *peoples* in this world who need to be reached with the gospel, but there are also unreached places in our hearts that still need to be reached with the gospel.

God sees every sin in our hearts and yet still loves us with all of his heart.

Few of us struggle to believe that God sees every part of our hearts, because that reality is fairly easy for us to grasp. The greater struggle comes when we are called to believe that God sees every sin in our hearts and yet still loves us with all of his heart.

If you are feeling discouraged and beginning to lose heart, I urge you to confront your unbelief. Let God's words in Jeremiah 32:41 herald God's heart to you: "I will rejoice in doing them good, and I will plant them in this land in faithfulness, with all my heart and all my soul."

God doesn't merely tolerate you, and he does not love you with half his heart. Instead, he loves you with all of his infinite heart and soul. Let the unreached places in your heart hope again!

PART TWO

—— ••• ——

HOW TO
DEFEAT DESPAIR

WHENEVER WE BEGIN TO LOSE HEART, we should take the gospel and press it into the deep places in our hearts where discouragement loves to hide. A thorough spring-cleaning will help us clear those hard-to-reach areas of our homes, and in the same way, a deep cleaning of our hearts will allow the gospel to do its work wherever discouragement can be found.

Why is discouragement so prevalent in our lives? In part 2, we will do a real-life assessment that examines the three tenses of discouragement. The past tense of discouragement is shame or bitterness about what we have done. The present tense of discouragement is disappointment about what we currently have. The future tense of discouragement is anxiety about what might happen in the future.

In the next three chapters, we will look at these three tenses and diagnose their root causes. Chapter 4 analyzes the past tense of discouragement as a memory problem, chapter 5 sees the present tense of discouragement as an expectation problem, and chapter 6 looks at the future tense of discouragement as an imagination problem. We will defeat these half-truths once again by seeing that the reasons to take heart are greater than the reasons to lose heart.

FOUR

What to Do When the Past Paralyzes You

I HAVE BEEN married for nineteen years, and I have many happy memories about the relationship I have with my wife. Cara is my best friend by far. We especially enjoy looking back and reliving some of our favorite dates together. One of my favorite memories is from the time I found out that she had once dreamed about being in the air force. By that point in our relationship, I had learned to plan dates that we would both enjoy rather than dates that only I would enjoy—no extra charge for that little piece of advice. One of my close friends was a pilot, and I asked him if he could take us flying. He delivered in a big way. He flew us to a nearby regional airport, I took her to a Mexican restaurant, and he flew us back. I have a picture of Cara and me standing next to the plane, and we both have beaming smiles. I love to look at that picture and relive the date.

Memories can be such a precious gift that allow us to enjoy the same event multiple times.

But our memories can also be a curse. One of the most painful moments of my life came during premarital counseling. I tearfully told Cara (my fiancée at that time) about some of my past pornography usage. By God's grace, pornography was no longer a problem in my life, but it was an issue in my past. I wanted her to know the truth about my old struggle, and I earnestly desired her forgiveness for that sin. I will never forget seeing the pain etched on her face. She freely forgave me, but it was a heart-wrenching experience for both of us.

For several days, I struggled to forgive myself. I was not applying the gospel to my situation. I wanted to beat myself up. I remembered the pain on Cara's face, and I replayed it in my mind over and over. I raked myself over the coals again and again for the bad choices I had made years before.

The Problem: We Twist the Time Machine of Memory

Our memories can serve as a kind of time machine. The time machine of memory can be a good thing when we go back and replay the good times because using it in this way can help us to enjoy a pleasant experience in exponential ways. But the time machine of memory becomes twisted when we use it to relive our past failures and punish ourselves multiple times for the same mistake. When we put our sins on repeat mode, we wince and groan over and over again because it triggers sharp pangs of guilt and shame. Our guilt brings past sins into the present and says, "Look, you *made* a mistake." Then shame joins the conversation and adds, "And you *are* the mistake."

Why do we torture ourselves by going back to the place of failure in our memory banks? Why do we continue to push the Play button and experience it all over again? We wish we could go back and erase our failures, but that's not an option. We cannot seem to *get* over it, so we *go* over it in our minds again and again.

Our problem is not that we look back but that we don't look all the way back.

Here is the problem with the twisted time machine of memory. We travel back in time under the pretense of a half-truth. Yes, we sinned, and sin should not be taken lightly. There is appropriate guilt and shame that come from sin, but as Christians, we know that "Christ Jesus came into the world to save sinners" (1 Tim. 1:15). We cannot allow our past shames to block the fact that Christ has come.

Discouragement gets stuck in the half-truth that says, "Go back and see for yourself that you failed," but we can take heart when we realize the full truth that our problem is not that we look back but that we don't look *all the way* back.

The Solution: Look All the Way Back

Yes, "the wages of sin is death" (Rom. 6:23), but our debts have been paid. Don't sit in your sin. Take it on a journey all the way back to the cross and see it nailed there.

I can remember the liberating moment when I stopped reliving my failures and raking myself over the coals and started looking at the cross instead. At the cross, God covered the sin of my pornography addiction with the blood of Jesus Christ. The wages of my sin have been paid in full.

When I finally turned my focus to the cross, the half-truth of discouragement gave way to the full truth of my total forgiveness. The half-truth of discouragement says our sin is only nailed to the cross "in part," but the truth of God's Word says our sin has been paid in full! The victory shout should well up within us as we sing the hymn, "It is Well with My Soul!"

> My sin—oh, the bliss of this glorious thought!—
> My sin, *not in part but the whole,*

Is nailed to the cross, and I bear it no more,
Praise the Lord, praise the Lord, O my soul![1]

Check the score. Look back and see the finished work. Say, "It is well with my soul," and sing of our Savior's love.

Facing Your Past

If dwelling on past sins is a fight for you, you are in good company. The apostle Paul had to fight this battle as well. He gave us an example of how to process our pasts in 1 Timothy 1.

In his first letter to his protégé, Timothy, Paul admitted that he was once a "blasphemer, persecutor, and insolent opponent" (v. 13). He even regarded himself as the "foremost" of sinners (v. 15). If there was ever a person who could spend a lifetime beating himself up for his sins, it was the apostle Paul. He could have replayed the times he railed against Jesus as a blasphemer and against Christians as deranged followers of a dead man over and over again. He could have relived the time he spent watching and giving approval to the religious leaders who stoned Stephen to death (Acts 7:58; 8:1). He could have recounted the men and women he had seized and dragged out of their homes to be imprisoned for their faith in Jesus (Acts 8:3).

No one could match how fiercely Paul had been op-
posed to Christ and the church. We may not have exactly
the same past as Paul, but we all have a past. My guess is
that it is messy and the memory of it is still painful today.
Have the wounds of the past left a sore spot on your heart
that is tender to the touch? Sometimes bruises are easy to
see on the surface, but other times people have a deep tis-
sue wound that is far beneath the surface. The heavier the
hurts, the deeper the wound. It is easy to lose heart when
we are deeply wounded by the pain of our past. But Paul
tells us how to take the next step in healing after facing our
past. Let us take the next step with Paul.

Fully Accept the Truth

When Paul remembered his sin while writing to Timothy, a greater truth came rushing in to fill his entire frame
of vision. He declared,

> The saying is trustworthy and deserving of full acceptance,
> that Christ Jesus came into the world to save sinners, of
> whom I am the foremost. (1 Tim. 1:15)

Paul said this statement is both trustworthy and deserving of full acceptance. We should contemplate what both
of those affirmations really mean.

What does the term *trustworthy* signify? This is how I picture it: Imagine ice fishing season. Some of you may have a hard time picturing this if you have never attempted this unique activity, but I will try to make it clear. In some regions, it gets so cold that bodies of water develop a layer of ice thick enough that people can drive their trucks on top.

Early in the ice fishing season, people have to be careful because the ice is not very thick. Every year there are people who put their ice shacks on the lake when the ice is still too flimsy. There are even people who drive their trucks on the ice too soon and then the tow trucks have to do a different kind of fishing.

Paul's statement in 1 Timothy 1:15—that Christ has come to save sinners—has the same strength of a fully frozen lake that can hold trucks and people and anything else thrown upon it. This saying can hold up a semitruck without cracking. It is a trustworthy statement. Put the full weight of your trust in those words.

Paul's second affirmation is that Christ's coming to save sinners is "deserving of full acceptance" (v. 15). The fact of Christ's coming is so reliable that it not only *could* be accepted but *should* be accepted. But what type of acceptance does it deserve? The Savior's coming is so certain that the statement deserves full acceptance. Intellectual assent, partial acknowledgement, and half-hearted trust all fall short of what Christ's coming deserves and demands. It is so immensely true and massively important that it merits an eager and whole-hearted embrace.

Therefore, discouragement over past sins is a half-truth that refuses to fully accept that Jesus's death on the cross makes us "deserving of God's full acceptance." Discouragement sticks close to us because we only partially embrace the truth of the gospel. We struggle to embrace the good news because it seems almost too good to be true in full measure. God sent his Son. Jesus came into the world and suffered and died to save sinners. None of this work was half-hearted on God's part. Why should we receive it partially on ours? How difficult is it to fully accept the truth that Christ came to save sinners? It is a finished, fully trustworthy fact of our salvation. The Son of God left the heights of heaven and the courts of glory not as a reward for our righteousness but as a ransom for our sins.

Point Others to God's Mercy

On his journey of fully accepting the truth, Paul did not stop with his own salvation. When he replayed his past, Paul didn't end with Christ's mercy and his own encouragement. Instead, after he went back to the past, he returned to the present so drenched in mercy that he wanted others to share in that forgiveness as well.

Paul refused to get stuck in discouragement. He used his past to encourage not just himself but others as well. He went on to explain the full rationale for Christ's coming—not just to save himself but to use his story as an example for others.

> But I received mercy for this reason, that in me, as the foremost, Jesus Christ might display his perfect patience as an example to those who were to believe in him for eternal life (1 Tim. 1:16).

Christ's mercy made an example out of Paul. These days, we often hear the phrase "I will make an example out of him" used negatively. The person serving as the "example" receives a harsh punishment in order to deter others who might otherwise have considered doing the same things. It is like the captain of a pirate ship who forces someone to walk the plank while everyone else watches. They point to the person on the plank and say, "This is what will happen to anyone else who defies me."

But Christ's mercy served a positive purpose in Paul's life. Christ made Paul an example, not to deter people but to invite them to experience his mercy and eternal life. We can look at Paul and say, "This is what will happen to anyone else who receives Christ's mercy."

Paul stood under the shower of mercy, and all of his sins were washed away. The same mercy is available to all of us. If the grace of God's mercy can wash away the sins of the foremost sinner, then it can wash away all of our sins as well.

Praise God

The lessons we can learn from Paul don't stop there. The finale of faith is a song of praise.

To the King of the ages, immortal, invisible, the only God, be honor and glory forever and ever. Amen. (1 Tim. 1:17)

Do you see the process from beginning to end? What a sequence! Replaying the sins of our past should lead us to praise, not pity and discouragement. This realization can be a life-changing lesson.

When we use the time machine of memory correctly, we can look at the past and say, "Unfortunately it is true. I acted that way. I talked that way. I thought that way. But Christ came. He bled and died in my place. He took my blame and bore the consequences. My sin, not in part but in whole, was nailed to the cross and shall stay there. Yes, my sins are piled high, but thank God that his grace rose higher and abounded all the more. I love my Savior so very much because I have been forgiven of so very much."

Then we can take the gospel comfort we have received and become a comforter in the lives of others. Sharing our faith will feel less forced. When we refuse to lose heart, we can compellingly give a reason for the hope that is in us. We can say, "I am swimming in the streams of mercy now.

I am urging you to join me. These streams will never run dry. There is quite enough love and power and patience in Christ to shower you as well!"

The Eclipse of the Cross

When it comes to past sins, we often have to fight for sight. Sin can become bigger in our sight than the power of God, which causes it to eclipse our view of the cross.

The sin in question could be our own or it could be the sin of someone who has wronged us. When our own sin becomes bigger to us than the cross, we struggle with false guilt because we fail to apply the gospel and forgive ourselves. But when someone else's sin eclipses the power of the cross, bitterness takes over because we fail to apply the gospel and forgive them. Past sins should never eclipse the cross and cause us to lose sight of our Savior.

Past sins should never eclipse the cross and cause us to lose sight of our Savior.

When Our Sins Seem Bigger Than the Cross

The fact that we are sinners cannot be denied, but our sin is not greater than our Savior. The cross of Christ does not belong hidden behind an overblown vision of overpowering sin. It does not dwarf the cross because our sin has been nailed there already (Col. 2:14).

In our fight for sight, we strain to see more than half of the story. Our sin is great, but it is not greater than his grace. The full story is that "where sin increased, grace abounded all the more" (Rom. 5:20).

When we allow our sins to eclipse our view of the cross, we become vulnerable because our perception and reality do not match. We feel spiritually dirty instead of cleansed by the blood of the Lamb. We feel spiritually empty instead of spiritually full in Christ.

Consider the words of the apostle Paul in Colossians 2:10: "You have been filled in [Christ], who is the head of all rule and authority." This text does not ask about our feelings; it declares our identities. Paul will not let us picture ourselves as empty if we are in Christ because Christ is complete—he lacks nothing. And in him, we, too, are complete. How could we ever need more than Christ?

I love the tense of the verb in Colossians 2:10. Paul does not say that we *were* filled or we *will be* filled or we *are being* filled. He uses the perfect tense in the original language to say we *have been* filled. We were filled up when we were saved and unified with Christ, and we are still full because we are still united with Christ. There is no leak in the fullness of Christ, and thus there is no leak in our identity in Christ.

Let me give you an analogy that might help you understand. Early in our married life, my wife and I used to play a game—though it has become less common now that I use it as a sermon illustration! We would say, "Happy anniversary" not only every year but also every month. Each of us would try to be the first person to say it, even if it meant waking the other person up at midnight to say, "Happy three-month anniversary!" We also would add, "I love you," and the other person, with a twinkle in their eye, would say, "I love you more." This response usually led to a silly game that went something like this: "Oh, that is the way you want to play. Well, then, let the games begin. I love you ten times more." "I love you a billion times more." The game would continue until one of us would say, "I love you infinity." We had to stop there. We could not pull a Buzz Lightyear and say, "To infinity and beyond!" We couldn't say, "I love you infinity plus ten," and so forth. That is not romantic; it's just bad math.

In the same way, it is also bad theology to say that we have Christ but we need a grace booster. Our salvation is not like a vitamin deficiency. The Bible tells us that in Christ, we have "all the fullness of God" (Eph. 3:19; Col. 1:19).

Many Christians struggle with an identity deficiency because they struggle to see their Savior through their view of sin. Therefore discouragement is a form of identity theft.

We do not *achieve* our identity in Christ; we *receive* it because it was purchased for us at the cross. However, when our sin becomes bigger than the cross, our sin becomes our identity.

Let's start fighting identity theft. As Christians, we are not living *for* an identity but *from* an identity. For example, when we are fighting the sin of anger, we allow it to become our identity when we say, "I am an angry person." In contrast, we testify to our true identity when we say, "I am a child of God in Christ who sometimes struggles with anger." Those two statements are similar but stunningly different in their understanding of the cross of Christ.

The same dynamic is true when it comes to traumatic events from our pasts. Someone close to me once confessed that after she went through a divorce, she felt as if she was walking around with a big fat *D* on her forehead. She felt like the divorce defined her. It became bigger than the cross because she thought everyone looked at her through that lens. People do similar things with anger or lust or worry.

It's essential for us to look at the clarity that the cross brings us at this point. Colossians 2:13–14 says that God took the record of debt, or the charges against us, and removed it by "nailing it to the cross." In Paul's day, the charge against a criminal was nailed above their cross upon crucifixion. Our charges were nailed to the cross and they no longer define us.

What gives us the right to try to take our record of debt back down and stamp it to our foreheads when Christ died so that we could be set free from it? Rather than remove the charge from the cross and stamp it again to our foreheads, let's choose to recall that God has removed our sins "as far as the east is from the west" (Ps. 103:12). In Christ, we are not only walking to victory (we have yet to experience it fully) but we are also walking from victory (Christ has defeated our sins).

I want to make one more important and necessary clarification. We do not need to minimize sin and spin the situation to put ourselves in the best possible light. If our sin has been nailed to the cross—not in part, but the whole—then we can own it all instead of minimizing all of it or denying some of it.

Let's say that you experienced a conflict in which the other person was significantly more at fault. Even if you were only 10 percent of the problem, you can own 100 percent of the blame because Christ paid for all of it. Forgiven sinners can become lead repenters rather than skilled pretenders.

Sin should grieve us to the core and stir us to respond in repentance. In 2 Corinthians 7:10, Paul distinguishes between godly grief and worldly grief: "Godly grief produces a repentance that leads to salvation without regret, whereas worldly grief produces death."

Worldly grief is a shallow sorrow. It is self-centered and feels remorse only when we have to suffer consequences because we cannot hide it anymore. A person experiencing worldly grief over sin may offer an apology, but that is not the same as repentance.

Unlike the self-centered sorrow of worldly grief, God-centered sorrow breaks our hearts. A person experiencing godly grief is broken over all of their sin, even sins of the heart that no one sees except God. God–centered grief confesses sins *specifically*, including sins of the heart. Godly grief over sin does not offer blanket apologies, such as "I'm sorry I did that." There is a greater specificity of confession because there is a greater sensitivity to sin.

Sorrow over our sin can be a good thing but only if we distinguish between conviction and condemnation. The Spirit uses conviction as a surgeon's scalpel to heal us. Satan uses condemnation as a weapon to wound us. The Spirit brings conviction for our sin so that we will repent and confess and receive forgiveness. Satan whispers condemning thoughts about our sin in an effort to make sin big, Christ small, and grace invisible. He aims to inflict multiple stab wounds to our hearts using the lies of condemnation. Satan continually tries to wield the weapon of false guilt, but he is a liar. The children of God know that "there is therefore now no condemnation for those who are in Christ Jesus" (Rom. 8:1).

When the Sins of Others Seem Bigger Than the Cross

We often give lip service to the virtue of forgiveness, but the reality is that granting forgiveness is easier said than done. Author and theologian C. S. Lewis put it well when he said, "Every one says forgiveness is a lovely idea, until they have something to forgive."[2] What do we do when the twisted time machine of memory takes us back to times when other people sinned against us?

Let me give a word of caution at the outset of this discussion about forgiveness. Do not confuse forgiving someone with trusting someone. For example, you can forgive a child molester, but that does not mean you are obligated to let him or her back into your life. Forgiveness is not earned, but trust is.

Why is it important to know that forgiveness is not something to be attained? When we say forgiveness is earned, we are saying the sins of others were not covered on the cross. We lose sight of the fact that our own forgiveness was not earned. The struggle here is that the sins of others can grow so large in our perspective that the cross is hidden from our sight. This eclipse of the cross puts us in eternal danger.

In Matthew 18, Jesus told a parable that warned us of the danger of not forgiving others. In this parable, he shared the story of a compassionate king who demonstrated forgiveness.

The kingdom of heaven may be compared to a king who wished to settle accounts with his servants. When he began to settle, one was brought to him who owed him ten thousand talents. And since he could not pay, his master ordered him to be sold, with his wife and children and all that he had, and payment to be made. So the servant fell on his knees, imploring him, "Have patience with me, and I will pay you everything." And out of pity for him, the master of that servant released him and forgave him the debt. (vv. 23–27)

It would have been shocking to Jesus's listeners that the king forgave such an impossibly large debt. It is difficult for us to calculate figures from ancient currency to a modern equivalent, but our best estimate is that a denarius was a coin that represented a day's work for a typical agricultural worker or skilled laborer. A talent was a unit of monetary reckoning equal to six thousand denarii (or six thousand days' wages). So ten thousand talents—roughly equal to sixty million days' wages—was an absurd amount of money. Just to show how high the number is, compare it to what the Jewish historian Josephus tells us about the taxes collected by the sons of Herod the Great upon his death. The taxes collected in all of Perea, Galilee, Batanaea, Trachonitis, Auranitis, Judea, Idumea, and Samaria equaled nine hundred talents—or 220 million dollars in modern currency. The servant in Jesus's parable owed ten times as much!

It is an unthinkable amount. The *Zondervan Illustrated Bible Backgrounds Commentary* says that ten thousand talents would equal about 2.5 billion dollars in today's currency.[3] The ESV Study Bible puts the amount around 6 billion dollars.[4] Jesus uses this financial figure to show that the amount is astronomical. The English word *zillions* is an equivalent term to get the point across.

Forgiving this debt would have been incredibly expensive for the king. Debts don't just go away; they have to be absorbed. If someone borrows something expensive and then accidentally breaks it, there are three options. The original owner can demand that the borrower pay to repair or replace the item, they each could pay for part, or the original owner could forgive the borrower and absorb the loss either by buying a new one or learning to live without whatever it was. Ten thousand talents was an unfathomably large amount for the king to absorb.

After the debtor had his enormous debt forgiven by the king, the scene shifted. We learn that this forgiven servant was owed a debt by someone else.

> When that same servant went out, he found one of his fellow servants who owed him a hundred denarii, and seizing him, he began to choke him, saying, "Pay what you owe." So his fellow servant fell down and pleaded with him, "Have patience with me, and I will pay you." He refused

and went and put him in prison until he should pay the debt. (Matt. 18:28–30)

What a stark contrast between the compassion of the king and the callousness of the servant! Someone who had been forgiven an insurmountable amount immediately went and choked someone who owed him something much less. What is striking is that Jesus says the servant "found" his fellow servant. This wording implies that he took initiative. The servant went looking for the person who owed him money and seized him. He became judge, jury, and torturer when he passed judgment and began to choke his fellow servant.

The indebted servant pleaded for mercy in nearly identical terms as the first servant had done, but it was to no avail. The words are chilling: "He refused." The plea for mercy fell on deaf ears and a hard heart.

We cultivate an unforgiving spirit when we allow someone else's sin to become bigger to us than the cross.

It seems ludicrous that someone could receive forgiveness for such a great debt and then go out of his way to try to force someone else to pay a small debt. But isn't that the heart of our problem? If we are not careful, this story can become our story. We cultivate an unforgiving spirit when we allow someone else's sin to become bigger to us than the cross. The sin of someone else eclipses the cross and hides it from our sight.

The problem is our perspective. The true picture looks like this:

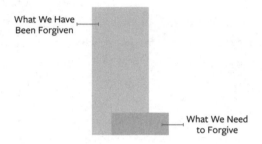

What We Have Been Forgiven

What We Need to Forgive

Unforgiveness is a reversal of reality. In our perspective, the debt others owe us seems bigger than the debt we owe God.

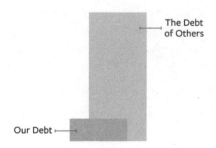

The Debt of Others

Our Debt

Our debt to God was incalculably bigger than anyone else's debt to us. The only way unforgiveness can flourish in our hearts is if we keep feeding the wrong done against us so that it grows in our sight. We let the magnitude of our sin and the wonder of the gospel shrink down to almost nothing. We need to come back to the reality of the cross and reflect on the horror of eternal unforgiveness in a place called hell.

Jesus did not pull any punches at the end of the story. He finished by sharing what will happen to those who callously choose not to forgive their fellow brothers and sisters.

> When his fellow servants saw what had taken place, they were greatly distressed, and they went and reported to their master all that had taken place. Then his master summoned him and said to him, "You wicked servant! I forgave you all that debt because you pleaded with me. And should not you have had mercy on your fellow servant, as I had mercy on you?" And in anger his master delivered him to the jailers, until he should pay all his debt. So also my heavenly Father will do to every one of you, if you do not forgive your brother from your heart. (Matt. 18:31–35)

Notice that the king called the servant "wicked." The word *all* is pointed. He said, "I forgave you *all* that debt" (Matt. 18:32). His mercy should have become the measure with which the forgiven servant related to others.

The next verse is a horror story: "And in anger his master delivered him to the jailers, until he should pay all his debt"

(Matt. 18:34). The word *jailers* has the overtone of *torturer*. The master handed over the servant to be tortured until "all his debt" was paid. This is a terrifying verse when we take into account the greatness of the debt he owed. Remember, his debt was equal to sixty million days of work—an impossible feat to overcome. Here we see the echoes of eternal debt and eternal punishment. Hell is a horror story with no closing credits.

Think of what is at stake if we refuse to forgive others. Unforgiveness is like a boomerang that comes back and hits us hard in the end. As speaker and author Bert Ghezzi once said it is like drinking poison and expecting the other person to die.[5] Unforgiveness is a cancer that eats away at us from the inside. A person with an unforgiving spirit has lost sight of God. In fact, an unforgiving spirit is an attitude that is in active opposition to God. Unforgiveness holds a grudge against the Judge.[6]

Let's take a moment to call this grudge to account. If a believer sins against you, and you are unwilling to forgive that person, then what you are really saying is this: "God, I don't like the way you run the universe. You need to do more." Can you hear the Father cross-examine your grudge? He looks at you and asks, "Are you really saying that the excruciating death of my beloved Son is not enough?"

In the same way, if you are unwilling to forgive an unbeliever who has sinned against you, then your actions are saying, "God, I disagree with the way you are dealing with this situation. You need to do it differently." God's response is still the same: "Do you really think that eternal torment in hell is not enough to punish this sin against you?"

We are free to forgive those who sin against us and not hold a grudge against the Judge.

The bottom line is this: All sin is first and foremost against God. The psalmist reminds us, "Against you, you only, have I sinned and done what is evil in your sight" (Ps. 51:4). God hates sin more intensely than we ever could. His coming judgment against sin will also be perfect and complete. Every sin will be judged. We can either accept that the Son of God has paid for it as our substitute on the cross or we will pay for it personally in hell. In both cases we are free to forgive those who sin against us and not hold a grudge against the Judge.

No Fishing

One precious woman from the first congregation I pastored often shared with others about how she had been set free by walking in the truth of God's forgiveness. She said that her favorite verse was Micah 7:19.

He will again have compassion on us;
    he will tread our iniquities underfoot.
You will cast all our sins
    into the depths of the sea.

She would recite that verse from memory and remind me that she believed that God buried our sin in the depths of the sea and remembered our sin no more. Then she would hurriedly add, "And when he buries our sin in the depths of that sea, he posts a sign that says, NO FISHING." That phrase was not a shallow, clever cliché for her. Sometimes she said it with a grin, other times she said it through tears, but it was never a tired cliché.

How about us? Christ did not save us so that we could become fishers of sin. Let's resolve to put our past in the past. At the cross, God put all our sins—and all the sins of others against us—under the blood of Jesus Christ. He buried them in the depths of the sea. Keep them there. No fishing.

FIVE

What to Do When the Present Disappoints You

I CAN REMEMBER one Christmas from my childhood when I was really into Transformers. That same year, my grandma asked me to pick out a toy from the JCPenney catalog for Christmas. There were two Transformers that I really wanted, and I could not choose between them. One transformed into a tank and a fighter plane while the other transformed into a train and a space shuttle. I had a tough time choosing because I could think of many different scenarios that each of these Transformers could fulfill. I needed a tank to man the bad guys' army, because the good guys already had a tank on their side, but I also needed a space shuttle for times when I needed to transport the other

Transformers into space to find energon cubes—let's just say I had an active imagination! Having to choose between the two toys had me so stumped that I finally told my grandma to surprise me.

Christmas Day finally came, and it was time to open the present from my grandparents. When I tore through the package, to my surprise, both Transformers were there! I squealed with delight and gave them both the biggest hugs imaginable. I was a happy little boy because my expectations had been doubly exceeded.

I received another present from my grandpa and grandma the next year. I ripped open the wrapping paper and eagerly looked inside the box, but it was just a pair of black socks. My parents must have seen the look of disappointment on my face, because they quickly told me to thank my grandparents. I dutifully muttered, "Thank you," even though I was far from grateful for my newest gift.

What happened in these two circumstances? In the first, I was extra joyful because my expectations had been exceeded. In the second, I was discouraged because I had expected a great gift like the year before, but instead I got black socks. To a ten-year-old, socks are pretty close to the worst gift ever. My expectations for that second year were high, and the reality of what I received was dismally low. As a result, I suffered sore disappointment.

The Problem: We Have Unmet Expectations

We have all tasted the joy of having our expectations exceeded, and we have all walked through the disappointment of unmet expectations. As we attempt to understand the effect our expectations have on our discouragement, perhaps it would be helpful to chart what disappointment looks and feels like.

Disappointment is the distance between what we expect and what we experience.

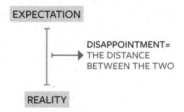

That principle plays out in the gap between the life we expected to have and the life we actually have.

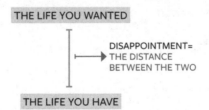

There are thousands of self-help books available today that tell people how to create the life they want, but the

Bible does not speak that way at all. Can you imagine telling the people of the persecuted church to read a book about *Disappointment* living their best life? The Bible takes us *is the distance* out of the here and now and gives us the *between what we* full picture so that we can fight for sight *expect and what* with the eyes of eternity. I describe how *we experience.* the apostle Paul skillfully helps us see the bigger picture in the next section.

The Solution: Look toward the Bigger Picture

Look at the way the apostle Paul brought eternity into the conversation about expectations.

> For this light momentary affliction is preparing for us an eternal weight of glory beyond all comparison, as we look not to the things that are seen but to the things that are unseen. For the things that are seen are transient, but the things that are unseen are eternal. (2 Cor. 4:17–18)

In this passage, Paul completely flipped the scales. He saw the affliction, but he did not lose heart because he chose to focus on the things that are eternal. Similarly, when we go through trials, we must compare our present sufferings ("the things that are seen") with our future glory, which cannot be seen.

Martyn Lloyd-Jones helps us see this picture in more detail. Lloyd-Jones asks us to picture the apostle Paul at his writing table, looking at a balance—a pair of scales with a pan on each side. As he looks at the balance, Paul pictures putting all his problems and troubles in one pan. The pan sinks under the weight of all those tribulations. But then Paul does something else. He takes hold of a "far more exceeding and eternal weight of glory" and puts it in the other pan. Lloyd-Jones explains,

> The learned commentators will tell you that at this point Paul's language fails him. He piles superlative on top of superlative, and still he cannot say it. A "far more," an "exceeding," an exceedingly abundant "weight of glory." He puts that on the other side. What happens? Down goes the pan, and that first weight was nothing. He does not say that it was light in and of itself but that when you contrast it with this "far more exceeding and eternal weight of glory" on the other side it becomes nothing. Put fifty-six pounds on one side—and it is a great weight. Yes, but put the "far more exceeding and eternal weight of glory" on the other side and your ton becomes a feather.[1]

Paul helps us comprehend the weight of glory by comparing it to the pain of the present. Contrasts are essential for gathering a proper perspective so we can understand the scope or magnitude of something. I once was scrolling through some pictures of our family vacation to Montana. One picture showed a mountain peak in the distance. It towered above its surroundings, but I did not fully grasp its immensity until I saw the next picture that showed a person at the bottom of the peak. The height of the mountain seemed even more staggering because I could instantly compare it to the size of the tiny person standing at its base.

Paul puts the weight of glory into perspective with a reference to our current sufferings. Those sufferings are "light" and "momentary" in comparison to the glory that is heavy ("the weight") and everlasting ("eternal"). The problem we face is that our trials feel far from light or temporary.

How do we fight this feeling? It is a fight for sight to look beyond present suffering and see future glory. In other words, we need the type of sight that can put things in their proper perspective and scope.

Affliction often feels overwhelming and unending rather than light and brief. In fact, Paul used the same Greek word for "affliction" that he used earlier. "We do not want you to be unaware, brothers, of the *affliction* we experienced in Asia" (2 Cor. 1:8).

The next phrase shows us that this affliction did not feel light and momentary to Paul. It felt so heavy that he was led to despair. "We were so utterly burdened beyond our strength that we despaired of life itself. Indeed, we felt that we had received the sentence of death" (2 Cor. 1:8–9).

These verses offer an important lesson. Two words in 2 Corinthians 1:8 reappear in 2 Corinthians 4:17: *affliction* and *weight* or *burden*. The affliction was an excessive burden when viewed on its own, but the matter changed for Paul when he weighed his present affliction against his future glory. When they were both set on the scales, the weight of glory launched

> *When affliction is all we see, we lose sight of eternity.*

all of his afflictions out of sight. A professional basketball player may seem really tall compared to a person of average height. We would not say the basketball player is short, but compared to a mountain, the basketball player may seem incredibly tiny. In the same way, our afflictions are only light and momentary in comparison to our future glory.

See Present Suffering in Light of Future Glory

When affliction is all we see, we lose sight of eternity. It is easy to get so immersed in this life that we lose sight of the life to come. We get so caught up in the view from below that we fail to see the view from above.

I am always amazed how different things look from an airplane or the top of a mountain. The things that seem so large and sprawling from the ground look small and compact from high in the sky. The same dynamic applies to time. This focus on the here and now can become so overwhelming that it shrinks our view of eternity. The solution, Lloyd-Jones says, is to resize eternity.

> There is only one thing to do with time, and that is to take it and put it into the grand context of eternity. When you and I look forward, ten years seems like a terribly long time. A hundred years? Impossible. A thousand? A million? We cannot envisage it. But try to think of endless time, millions upon millions upon millions of years. That is eternity. Take time and put it into that context. What is it? It is only a moment. If you look at time merely from the standpoint of your calendars and your almanacs and life as you know it in this world, it is an impossible tyranny. But put it into God's eternity and it is nothing.[2]

We don't lose heart when we suffer, Paul told us, because the suffering we see now serves the future glory we cannot see (2 Cor. 4:17). This eternal perspective does not make our present suffering meaningless but meaningful. We can endure our present suffering in light of its link to our future glory.

Few things can be as discouraging as pointless pain. When we go through tough times, one of our fears is that our suffering will be for no purpose. We want to think good will come out of it, but we don't see how. We fear that what we went through was all for nothing, but the Bible rebukes that half-truth. Yes, our suffering is painful. It's true that we cannot always see what it is doing now, but the fact that suffering is painful does not negate the fact that it is meaningful. We can say with the authority of heaven that, in Christ, our suffering is definitely not meaningless.

Our suffering is definitely not meaningless.

Paul said the affliction we see "*is preparing* for us" the glory we can't yet see but will see one day (2 Cor. 4:17). When we are going through pain and loss, we must remember that our suffering is for a purpose. It is working. It is producing a peculiar glory that we will receive only because of our present pain. God is also using our hardships to build within us the kind of dependence upon him that will not wander away but walk close to him on the road to the heavenly city.

Therefore, present afflictions and future glory are not merely contrasted; they are interrelated. Our sovereign God has designed suffering to serve and produce our future glory.

I love the way that the Puritan preacher Lemuel Haynes put this principle into words.

Every pain, every tear, every insult they bear for Christ's sake will secure them a great reward in heaven (Matt. 5:12). The wearisome and tiresome nights they spend here in running their race and finishing their course will only prepare them for a more sweet repose and rest at their journey's end, when the morning shall break forth.[3]

Look to the Things That Are Unseen

What should we do when we are faced with suffering and trials? Paul gets really practical by telling us where our focus should be: "We look not to the things that are seen but to the things that are unseen. For the things that are seen are transient, but the things that are unseen are eternal" (2 Cor. 4:18).

We don't lose heart when we know where to fix our eyes. Evaluating our sufferings based only on what can be seen leads to a distorted picture, because there is more to the story than what is immediately visible. Pain demands our attention and screams to be our sole focus. We don't lose heart because we don't allow our pain to divert our attention away from the clear truth that the tangible is temporary and the immaterial is eternal.

Our sovereign God has designed suffering to serve and produce our future glory.

Focusing on the things that are unseen is easier said than done because tangible things seem more real than immaterial things. On the other hand, tangible things are temporary. We don't want to base our future on that which won't exist in the future. The unseen things are harder to grasp, but they are eternal. Walking by faith is difficult because we have to work hard to keep the things that can't be seen in view.

C. S. Lewis commented on the painful effort required to see eternal things.

> The real problem of the Christian life comes where people do not usually look for it. It comes the very moment you wake up each morning. All your wishes and hopes for the day rush at you like wild animals. And the first job each morning consists in shoving them all back; in listening to that other voice, taking that other point of view, letting that other larger, stronger, quieter life come flowing in. And so on, all day. Standing back from all your natural fussings and frettings; coming in out of the wind.
>
> We can do it only for moments at first. But from those moments the new sort of life will be spreading through our system: because now we are letting Him work at the right part of us. It is the difference between pain, which is merely laid on the surface, and a dye or stain which soaks right through.[4]

I want to help you in the painful effort to keep the reasons to take heart in view.

Seeing and Longing in the Light of Eternity

When we go through times of trials and suffering, how do we listen to that other voice and keep an eternal perspective in view?

See What Is Really There and Respond Appropriately

The world we live in is fallen, yet it is our Father's world. In this fallen world, there are signs of death, decay, and destruction all around us, but there are also signs of grace, goodness, and beauty. We must take the time to see them both and then respond in a way that fits each one.

We should lament the things in this world that are broken and bad and sinful. We should grieve. This brokenness reminds us that sin runs counter to God's good design. As Christians, we are not called to be stoics. Christianity is not a fantasyland filled with imaginary things that do not correspond to reality. It is not a form of escapism, like making up an imaginary friend because we are lonely.

Christians must guard against adopting the glib perspective that I call the "Pollyanna Principle." The main character in the 1960 Disney movie adaptation of *Pollyanna* always tried to find the positive side in everything. There is nothing wrong with seeing the glass half full, but there is no virtue in being excessively optimistic to the point that you become blind to the real pain that surrounds you. See the things that sting. Don't ignore them. Don't try to pretend they aren't there.

We should also savor and celebrate the things that are good and true and beautiful and sweet in this world. God reveals much of himself through his creation. Paul tells us that God's "eternal power and divine nature, have been clearly perceived, ever since the creation of the world, in the things that have been made" (Rom. 1:20). It is important to recognize God's blessings in our world and celebrate that "every good gift and every perfect gift is from above" (James 1:17).

The demons want to distort this picture and make God look like a *forbidder* rather than a *creator* and *giver*. Paul points to this demonic distortion in 1 Timothy 4:1–5.

> In later times some will depart from the faith by devoting themselves to deceitful spirits and teachings of demons, through the insincerity of liars whose consciences are seared, who forbid marriage and require abstinence from foods that God created to be received with thanksgiving by those who believe and know the truth. For everything created by God is good, and nothing is to be rejected if it

is received with thanksgiving, for it is made holy by the word of God and prayer.

Demons teach that enjoyable things, such as marriage and certain foods, should be forbidden. Demons are false teachers that depict a false god who takes pleasure in twisted things. In this false teaching, their so-called creator plays a sick trick on his creatures. He creates pleasant things and then forbids people from finding pleasure in them. That is not just lame; it is sick and wrong. No surprise there—the teaching is evil because the source is evil.

Our ability to enjoy all that God made rests on our distinction between structure and direction. The Bible tells us that "everything created by God is good" (1 Tim. 4:4). These good things, such as food, sex, and music can be taken in God-ward directions that bring glory to God and joy to people, or they can be taken in godless directions that dishonor God and hurt people. Christians should lead the way in showing how to enjoy God-honoring delight in all that God has made.

Christians should lead the way in showing how to enjoy God-honoring delight in all that God has made.

Historically the church has been quick to focus on the danger of materialism or overindulgence when it comes to creation. The church, however, has been slower to attack underindulgence with respect to creation. Underindulgence, sometimes called asceticism, is something that the church has often failed to identify as an enemy of the gospel. In 1 Timothy 4, Paul said that asceticism is a departure from faith.

Self-denial is a denial of the gospel because it makes our denial of good things part of the gospel. It is a departure from our faith when we try to use our self-denial to achieve acceptance with God. It can become easy to start trusting in our self-denial as if it is pleasing to God. We think, "The more I give up, the more impressed God is with me. Look how much of God's stuff I am saying no to!" Why on earth would we think that God would be impressed when we say no to the very gifts that he has given us?

Imagine a home in which a loving father packs a lunch for his child every day. One particular morning, the dad gets up extra early to make an extra-special lunch for his child. He smokes some fall-off-the-bone barbecue ribs. He makes extra-cheesy macaroni. As he packs the lunch, he cannot stop smiling as he thinks about how much his child will enjoy the special meal. Later that day, when the dad picks his child up after school, he asks with a twinkle in his eye, "So what did you think of the special lunch I made you?"

Now imagine the child saying, "Daddy, I have a wonderful surprise for you. I threw most of it away!"

The dad's jaw drops. "What?"

The child says, "Yeah, I thought about how good it would taste, but then I thought about how pleased you would be with my self-control and willpower to resist. Aren't you impressed by how much of the lunch I was able to get rid of? Aren't you proud of me?"

What would the dad say? I know I would say something like, "How does that please me? I feel dishonored. I delighted in the gift I gave you, and you completely missed the point. I didn't give you food so you could turn it into a self-centered feat of self-control. I prepared it for you to enjoy. You want me to praise you for saying no to the feast I gave you? I wanted you to be full and happy and thankful, not prideful and boastful."

So here is the application: Enjoy God's enjoyable gifts. Really, I mean it. Really, truly enjoy them. Get every ounce of joy out of every ounce of a Dove dark chocolate ice cream bar or a sunny afternoon on the lake. While you are at it, teach your kids how to enjoy God's creation.

In my family, we have something called TNT (Treats 'n' Talking). This is a time when we gather to chat with one another while indulging in something sweet, like root beer floats. My wife and I are teaching our kids how to know the God "who richly provides us with everything to enjoy" (1 Tim. 6:17). We call it TNT because we don't just enjoy treats; we enjoy each other. I hugged my kids and just enjoyed playing with them this week. It was great!

They do not think of their daddy as dour and sour. I love to have fun with them. I encourage you to enjoy the tangible blessings in your relationships.

Remember God Sees More Than You See

Seeing only the things that sting can cause us to become cynical. Many skeptics reason that God sees the things that are painful yet does not stop them; therefore, he must not be good. The logic goes like this: God *hasn't* done anything; therefore, he *won't* do anything. The solution to this problem is to remember that God sees not only the things we see but much, much more.

A few years ago a friend of mine went through a difficult season after he lost his job. Financial fears came rushing at him from all sides as he worried about what his family's future would look like if he could not provide for them. We prayed together, and I asked God to pour out a Romans 8:28 grace on him—that is, faith to lay hold of the promise that God was actually at work for both his good and the good of his family.

God answered that prayer through a series of events in my friend's life. He had a routine physical and discovered that his stress levels at his old job had made him a ticking time bomb as a heart attack candidate. That scary news forced my friend to slow down. He learned to operate at a different pace of life with more margin and less stress. He eventually landed a job that paid less, but he enjoyed it far more than his old position. He did not take his work home with him like before, and he ended up connecting with his children on a deeper level. God had indeed been at work for his good and the good of his family.

The loss of a job felt like the frown of God upon my friend's life. But God saw the pain and heartache too; he saw more than my friend could see. The days that followed the loss of his job began to reveal God's smiling face.

As William Cowper's famous hymn declares,

> Judge not the Lord by feeble sense,
> but trust him for his grace.
> Behind a frowning providence,
> he hides a smiling face.[5]

Discouragement can sometimes be a form of arrogance. It sets in when we take everything we see and add it up. If the sum total is high enough, we feel hope. If it dips below a certain level, we feel discouraged.

Yes, God sees what we see. He knows the circumstances and situations that leave us feeling discouraged. But that is no reason to allow hopelessness and cynicism to take root in our hearts. They will bear bitter fruits in our souls and choke away all hope from thinking what we see is *all that there is to see.* If we look too long at what is bitter, then we will become bitter.

Those feelings are finite, because we cannot see all that there is in store for us. God's vision is infinite. If we were to take his perspective, we would also adopt his outlook. The future does not look bleak to him, so it should not look bleak to us either. This is where trust is essential in our walks of faith.

Are we really so arrogant that we think we can see the whole picture? Faith comes when our hearts know that God sees what we see—and he also sees more than we see as well. He sees it all and knows it all because he wrote the future. Believe as Abraham did—be "fully convinced that God [is] able to do what he had promised" (Rom. 4:21).

God said that he is working all things together for the good of those who love him (Rom. 8:28). They are "glorified" (Rom. 8:30). Light and momentary afflictions are working for "an eternal weight of glory beyond all comparison" (2 Cor. 4:17). God is at work even when we don't see the purpose of our trials. Our present sufferings are serving up glory even when we do not comprehend the carving.

Look at Your Longings

The things that are wrong in this world and the things that are right in it both create eager longings. The things that are wrong and broken and twisted cause us to look forward to heaven, because we long for the day when our present sufferings will be things of the past. We want things to work right and not break down. That is true whether we are talking about our bodies or our cars or our relationships or our appliances.

But those longings do not fully fit in a world where things eventually break down and decay. Those are transposed longings—they show that our hearts are pointed heavenward. C. S. Lewis made the same point when he wrote, "If we find ourselves with a desire that nothing in this world can satisfy, the most probable explanation is that we were made for another world."[6]

Even the things that are good and true and beautiful here on earth can point our hearts toward heaven in worshipful wonder and eager longing. God's gifts are meant to be a means for us to enjoy God himself.

God's gifts are meant to be a means for us to enjoy God himself.

Don't use God as a steppingstone to get his gifts. Use his gifts as a stepping-stone to enjoy God. Think about how much more enjoyable the God who created these good things must be. If a root beer float is sweet, imagine how sweet God is as the all-surpassing fount of every good and perfect gift. All good things point to the Creator. He is the place from where all the goodness, truth, and beauty originate. C. S. Lewis can help us interpret our longings. He said, "It was when I was happiest that I longed most. . . . The sweetest thing in all my life has been the longing—to reach the Mountain, to find the place where all the beauty came from."[7]

When we taste the beauty, we can also trace it back to the One from whom it all came. Imagine what the things of earth will be like once God has restored earth to his original, perfect design. All the things that are wrong and broken will be gone. All the things that are good now will be beyond our wildest dreams. Creation is currently in bondage to corruption, but one day it will be set free. Paul described this reality in Romans 8.

> For the creation waits with eager longing for the revealing of the sons of God. For the creation was subjected to futility, not willingly, but because of him who subjected it, in hope that the creation itself will be set free from its bondage to corruption and obtain the freedom of the glory of the children of God. (vv. 19–21)

Why do we cry? We cry because everything in us screams, "Something went wrong." Everywhere we look, we see reasons to lose hope. The world can be a place of great delight, but it can also be a place that knocks the wind out of you just as quickly.

The wrong things in this world create in us an "eager longing" (v. 19) for the next world. Someday creation will finally be set free from its futility and slavery to corruption. Paul said that God subjected creation to slavery and decay in order to serve hope. Read those words again. "The creation was subjected to futility, not willingly, but because of him who subjected it, *in hope* that the creation itself will be set free from its bondage to corruption and obtain the freedom of the glory of the children of God" (vv. 20–21).

We are moving from slavery to freedom, from suffering to healing, from deterioration to new creation! The wrong serves the right by creating an eager longing for the latter. The Bible describes this present life as "sorrowful, yet always rejoicing" (2 Cor. 6:10), but a day is coming when we will be always rejoicing and never sorrowful. What will that be like? Creation is currently limited, but one day it will be set free from its bondage.

This idea reminds me of my dog, Kaiser. He loves to run. All I have to do is ask, "Do you want to go for a walk?" and he whines and paws at the door because he knows what is coming. But when he gets out, he is tethered by a leash. He has to run at my pace. I slow him down, so he strains against the leash. But when we get to the park, with its wide-open places to wander, I let him off the leash and watch him run like the wind with his ears back and tail up. It is worshipful to see him free to do exactly what God created him to do. In the same way, someday God will let creation off its leash. What a day that will be!

The Hope of Glory

I began this chapter by talking about a time when my expectations were doubly exceeded. Our future glory in heaven will infinitely exceed our expectations. The Bible speaks of future glory as something that we simply cannot fully anticipate or fathom ahead of time. This life will disappoint, but the life to come will exceed all of our expectations.

As we saw at the beginning of this chapter, our experience in this life often looks like this:

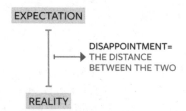

The life to come will gloriously turn disappointment on its head.

The world to come is a place where disappointment is impossible. Think about this: All of our expectations are finite, but God is infinite. It will be impossible for finite beings to be disappointed with the world an infinite being of pure love, perfect wisdom, and almighty power has prepared for us.

Take another look at the diagram of disappointment at the beginning of this chapter. Disappointment is the distance between what we expect and what we experience. The hope of glory turns disappointment upside down. In heaven, what we will experience will exceed our expectations to a superlative, immeasurable degree. We can set our hopes as high as possible, and we will still find that they are child's play compared to what God has prepared for us.

> *The world to come is a place where disappointment is impossible.*

SIX

What to Do When the Future Scares You

A FEW YEARS AGO, my family and I moved to Ethiopia for six months while we completed an adoption. I can remember how hard it was to set my expectations. There was a period of time when I found it hard to sleep because I would worry about certain scenarios.

For example, I had read that there were many people who would try to pickpocket foreigners. I began to imagine what it would be like to have my wallet stolen. What would I do? Would I race after the thief the minute I realized I had been robbed? What if I caught him and he didn't give it back? What would I do if I lost my passport or identification papers? My heart became an anxiety factory.

I began to come up with action plans for different scenarios. I would keep my wallet in my front pocket. Maybe I would buy some pants with zippers on the side. If people still managed to get my wallet, then I could be ready by having phone numbers to contact in case of an emergency.

Anxiety comes from an overactive heart and mind.

Maybe I would keep my money split up in different places so these imaginary offenders couldn't get all of it at once.

Imagination can be a gift, but it can also be a curse. We imagine what we will have to face in the future, and then our hearts and minds get involved in envisioning how we would respond to certain scenarios. Before we realize it, we are spending our time and energy responding to future scenarios that may never happen.

Anxiety comes from an overactive heart and mind.

The Problem: We Project Our Fears into the Future

We project our fears into the future and then imagine what we would do if we had to face them. Several theologians have diagnosed this dynamic. In his book *Spiritual Depression*, Martyn Lloyd-Jones saw these principles at work with an overactive heart and mind. Our imaginations confront us and ask a series of scenario questions, such as "What if this or that should happen?"[1] Then the heart is startled into anxiety and begins to study those scenarios and react to them by saying, "If that should take place we shall have to make this arrangement, or we shall have to do that."[2]

Many of us are familiar with the concept that having an overactive bladder causes you to go to the bathroom frequently, but where do we go with an overactive, anxious heart and mind?

The Solution: Look All the Way Ahead

When it comes to anxiety, we need to see the problem clearly. And the issue isn't that we look ahead, it's that we don't look *all the way* ahead. Instead of seeing things in light of eternity, we tend to focus our attention myopically on our immediate problems.

We need an eternal perspective or we become shortsighted. Why stop halfway at a place of uncertainty and difficulty? It is not wrong to go there, but it is wrong to stay there. The thing you are worried about may happen, but it also may not. Either way, it is definitely not what we should set our sights toward.

> *The issue isn't that we look ahead, it's that we don't look all the way ahead.*

Our heavenly Father is the author of our stories. He has already written every one of our days from birth to death. As the psalmist said, "In your book were written, every one of them, the days that were formed for me, when as yet there was none of them" (Ps. 139:16). Go ahead and read that again. He has written an everlasting conclusion for us in which every chapter is better than the last. The future is brighter than we can imagine; the best is yet to come.

The future is brighter than we can imagine; the best is yet to come.

The doctrine of heaven helps us not only die well someday but also live well today. Imagine a hypothetical future scenario that would elicit fear. For example, what if persecution comes and you lose your job, your financial well-being, even your home? The writer of Hebrews wrote to people who were facing the third scenario.

> For you had compassion on those in prison, and you joy-fully accepted the plundering of your property, since you knew that you yourselves had a better possession and an abiding one. (Heb. 10:34)

These Christians visited other believers in prison, know-ing that by doing so, they opened themselves up to the same persecution, even the plundering of their property. But these Christians also knew how to look all the way ahead and see the good gift that they could not lose. In this life, we can rest in the peace that Jesus has already fought for us, and we can rest in the assurance of our future with him. Our present rest and our future rest come together in Jesus Christ.

Thankfully, the same eternal perspective is as powerful today as it was in the first century. Not long ago, I read Nik Ripken's *The Insanity of God* and discovered this scenario story that shows what is happening to the persecuted church in China.

The security police regularly harass a believer who owns the property where a house-church meets. The police say, "You have got to stop these meetings! If you do not stop these meetings, we will confiscate your house, and we will throw you out into the street."

Then the property owner will probably respond, "Do you want my house? Do you want my farm? Well, if you do, then you need to talk to Jesus because I gave this property to Him."

The security police will not know what to make of that answer. So they will say, "We don't have any way to get to Jesus, but we can certainly get to you! When we take your property, you and your family will have nowhere to live!"

And the house-church believers will declare, "Then we will be free to trust God for shelter as well as for our daily bread."

"If you keep this up, we will beat you!" the persecutors will tell them.

"Then we will be free to trust Jesus for healing," the believers will respond.

"And then we will put you in prison!" the police will threaten.

By now, the believers' response is almost predictable: "Then we will be free to preach the good news of Jesus to the captives, to set them free. We will be free to plant churches in prison."

"If you try to do that, we will kill you!" the frustrated authorities will vow.

And, with utter consistency, the house-church believers will reply, "Then we will be free to go to heaven and be with Jesus forever."[3]

Jesus tells us not to be anxious about food and clothing because "all these things" will be added to us as we "seek first the kingdom of God and his righteousness" (Matt. 6:33). Jesus is describing the normative pattern of daily life. These things will be added to us, but persecuted believers know that in this world they can also be taken away from us. We may experience "tribulation, or distress, or persecution, or famine, or nakedness, or danger, or sword" (Rom. 8:35). The promise is not that we will never have to face these things but that God's love cannot be taken away. These things cannot separate us from God's love. We are "more than conquerors through him who loved us" (Rom. 8:37). Therefore we can share in Paul's certainty.

> For I am sure that neither death nor life, nor angels nor rulers, nor things present nor things to come, nor powers, nor height nor depth, nor anything else in all creation, will be able to separate us from the love of God in Christ Jesus our Lord. (Rom. 8:38–39)

I love that Paul adds "nor anything else in all creation." Whenever our anxious, overactive hearts and minds make us dwell on the uncertainty of the future, we can face those insecurities and ask, "Is this part of the 'anything else' of Romans 8:39?" The answer is yes. God promises that no matter what we face in life, it will not be able to separate us from the Father's love in Christ.

No matter what we face in life, it will not be able to separate us from the Father's love in Christ.

When we have an eternal perspective that has read ahead and knows how the story ends, it enables us to go back to the chapter that has us stuck. We do not put our hope in a better version of ourselves that can handle the future version of our problems. Instead, we "trust in the name of the Lord our God" (Ps. 20:7).

We are not on our own. God is at work. The grace needed to take us to heavenly glory will be there for us every day. If we are justified, then we are also glorified (Rom. 8:30). We are not orphans left to fend for ourselves. When we call out to our Father, he is there to listen.

New Morning Mercies

Why do we write our Father and his grace out of the story our imaginations have created for us? If we imagine hypothetical trouble, why do we have a hard time imagining guaranteed grace to go with it? We look at the future and act as if our troubles will be there but God's grace will not. We lose heart when we borrow tomorrow's trouble without also factoring in tomorrow's mercies.

Jesus analyzes our anxieties in the same way. He said, "Do not be anxious about tomorrow, for tomorrow will be anxious for itself. Sufficient for the day is its own trouble" (Matt. 6:34). When we are anxious, we are borrowing trouble from the future and adding it to today's trouble. We have an inborn tendency to look at the sum total of what we can see coming at us (potential or actual) and treat it like a lump-sum loan. We walk around feeling bankrupt because at any point we could be called to account and be declared bankrupt.

We have forgotten about the certainty of guaranteed grace described in Lamentations 3:21–24.

> But this I call to mind,
>> and therefore I have hope:
> The steadfast love of the LORD never ceases;
>> his mercies never come to an end;
> they are new every morning;
>> great is your faithfulness.
> "The LORD is my portion," says my soul,
>> "therefore I will hope in him."

Did you see why we can hope? God's love and his mercies do not run out. They are new every morning.

We become discouraged when we take the way that God works out of the equation. He does not give us a handful of grace upon our salvation and then ask us to use that amount, a little at a time, for the rest of our lives. No, God gives us what we need every day. His love and mercy never ends. He gives us an endless supply that never runs dry by making deposits of grace in our lives every morning without exception—great is his faithfulness!

Think about the foolish borrowing we do. We borrow trouble *from tomorrow* and try to pay for it with the grace we have *for today*. Of course there is not enough. God did not design it that way. He does not give us today the grace we need for tomorrow. Grace is like breathing. We cannot take in enough breath to cover what is needed for tomorrow. Likewise, we cannot eat enough food today to last the next few months. Breathing and eating are daily realities. Grace is the same way. A fresh supply of God's all-sufficient grace will arrive tomorrow for us to face tomorrow's troubles.

Cast Your Cares on the Father

Anxiety can sometimes be a form of arrogance. Pride tells us to carry our cares on our own instead of casting them on our Father. That is why the Bible says we humble ourselves by casting our cares on him (1 Pet. 5:6–7). Bring your cares to him in prayer. God's peace is the solution for an overactive, anxious heart and mind.

God's peace is the solution for an overactive, anxious heart and mind.

Look at how Paul described this practice in Philippians 4:6–7.

> Do not be anxious about anything, but in everything by prayer and supplication with thanksgiving let your requests be made known to God. And the peace of God, which surpasses all understanding, will guard your hearts and your minds in Christ Jesus.

Notice that we should bring our petitions to God with thanksgiving, which can come only when we bring our

Father back into the story. We should be thankful that God has not abandoned us to try to live this life on our own. Instead, he has promised to always be with us and to care for us.

I can remember when my daughter was learning to give to God financially. The lessons started with tithing. One week, she decided to put all of her money in the offering plate. I told her that it was fine to give all her money to God but she did not have to do so. She could keep some. She just looked at me for a moment and then said something that has always stuck with me: "Why do I need money? I have a daddy!" I have come back to this precious reminder time and time again. Why am I so worried? I have a Father!

That is why the Bible gives us a tender incentive for giving our cares to God: "[Cast] all your anxieties on him, *because he cares for you*" (1 Pet. 5:7). Jesus said that we are surrounded by examples of our Father's care every day.

> Look at the birds of the air: they neither sow nor reap nor gather into barns, and yet your heavenly Father feeds them. Are you not of more value than they? And which of you by being anxious can add a single hour to his span of life? And why are you anxious about clothing? Consider the lilies of the field, how they grow: they neither toil nor spin, yet I tell you, even Solomon in all his glory was not arrayed like one of these. But if God so clothes

the grass of the field, which today is alive and tomorrow is thrown into the oven, will he not much more clothe you, O you of little faith? Therefore do not be anxious, saying, "What shall we eat?" or "What shall we drink?" or "What shall we wear?" For the Gentiles seek after all these things, and your heavenly Father knows that you need them all. But seek first the kingdom of God and his righteousness, and all these things will be added to you. (Matt. 6:26–33)

In this passage, Jesus gave us two examples of God's attentive care for his creation: birds and flowers. Don't let the familiarity of this passage cause you to miss how ridiculous the word pictures really are as we look at the birds and the flowers.

Consider the Birds

Let's consider the birds first. Jesus said, "They neither sow nor reap nor gather into barns, and yet your heavenly Father feeds them" (Matt. 6:26). This point is stunningly obvious. No one has ever seen a sparrow driving a tractor with a tiller cultivating the field. A crow has never been spotted driving a combine to gather the harvest. You never see them planting or gardening! Birds don't sow seeds; they eat them.

How do the birds get food if they don't sow and reap? God takes care of them!

Look at how God reminds Job of his promises in Job 38:39–41.

> Can you hunt the prey for the lion,
>   or satisfy the appetite of the young lions,
> when they crouch in their dens
>   or lie in wait in their thicket?
> Who provides for the raven its prey,
>   when its young ones cry to God for help,
> and wander about for lack of food?

God goes on to confront Job with his supernatural care of the goats, the donkey, the bull, the ostrich, the warhorse, and the eagle. God's glory is on display in the way that he cares for his creatures.

God's point in the book of Job is to mercifully tear Job down from his lofty palace of pride; his point in Matthew is to lift us up from wallowing in the mud puddle of worry. So Jesus drives his point deep into the anxious hearts of his disciples: "Are you not of more value than they?" (Matt. 6:26). The answer is, "Of course you are more valuable than they are."

Jesus's rhetorical question uses a vertical scale of God's care toward his creation. Where do we rank in terms of

God's care for his creatures? Birds are on the scale some-where. I don't know what is below them—maybe slugs? But we do know what ranks far above both—we do! Humanity is the crown of God's creation.

Consider the Flowers

Jesus also tells us to look at the flowers of the field. "Why are you anxious about clothing? Consider the lilies of the field, how they grow: they neither toil nor spin, yet I tell you, even Solomon in all his glory was not arrayed like one of these" (vv. 28–29). Do you see his point? You never see flowers with a needle and thread or a sewing machine. They never have to knit or crochet. How do they have such a beautiful outer appearance? Because God clothes them. Even Solomon, perhaps the wealthiest man in the ancient world, could not dress himself as extravagantly as God dresses up the flowers. Give me a tulip festival over a royal processional any day.

Jesus gently confronts us as he describes the way God clothes the flowers. "But if God so clothes the grass of the field, which today is alive and tomorrow is thrown into the oven, will he not much more clothe you, O you of little faith?" (v. 30). Jesus's rhetorical question uses a horizontal scale of longevity. What is the life span of a flower? It lasts longer than a fruit fly but is much shorter than the life span of a human. The fact that humans live longer than flowers says something about God's great love for humanity. Will he devote less of his time and energy to something that he made in his image to last forever than he does to something he made that lasts only for a little while?

Consider the Cross

The end of Matthew's Gospel shows us the full extent of God's care. Jesus used the example of God's care of birds and flowers to show us God's love. The Gospels end with a focus on Jesus's death and resurrection as a demonstration of his love. "God so loved the world, that he gave his only Son, that whoever believes in him should not perish but have eternal life" (John 3:16). Yes, nature proves that God cares for his creation, but the gospel is also the greatest proof of God's care for us. There is no plan of salvation for birds or flowers. How much more is God's love and care displayed for us on the cross!

When we come to God with our thanksgiving and our petitions, we experience his promise of peace. He has not promised to fix our circumstances. Peace is not the absence of difficult circumstances; it is the presence of the Prince of Peace. He often deals with difficult circumstances not by taking them away but by giving us more of himself.

Worldly peace is something that we achieve and we guard. But God's peace is given. We don't guard it; it guards us.

Trust God with Tomorrow

I still remember the moment that these truths took hold of my heart with life-changing power. I was sitting in the sanctuary at a Wednesday night gathering at Bethlehem Baptist Church in April of 2009. We were watching a video about the persecuted church. In the video, we saw radical Muslims break into a Christian assembly of worship and put guns to the heads of the believers, demanding, "Renounce Christ or die!" The Christians did not renounce Christ, even in the face of death, so they were shot. My mind and heart jumped into hyperdrive— not just overactive but hyperactive. I wondered and worried in the quietness of that moment: *Would I be able to do that?*

God's peace is given. We don't guard it; it guards us.

After the video, Pastor John Piper came to the microphone and said, "Many of you are wondering if you could do that." He certainly had my attention. Piper continued, "The answer is no. You could not do it today because you have not been called to do it today. But if and when that day ever comes, God's grace will be there so that you can."[4]

When your imagination takes you into uncharted territory, bring these truths with you. God is the author of your story. Open God's Word and read ahead. The best is yet to come. When tomorrow arrives, God's grace will be there to take care of tomorrow's troubles.

Let's take our cares to God and trust him to calm our overactive hearts and minds and guard them with his peace.

CONCLUSION

God's Not Done

THE U.S. BANK STADIUM in Minneapolis, Minnesota, hosted the Super Bowl in 2018. Construction for the venue was completed in 2016. It was fascinating to watch the progress of the building throughout its assembly.

I used to drive by the stadium every week to see the progress. I couldn't believe how big of a hole they had to dig before they could start building. As the structure began to take shape little by little, it was hard to imagine what it would even look like. Back when it was just a hole in the ground, one of my colleagues at church asked our congregation how they liked the new stadium. It was meant to be a joke because, at that particular moment in time, one would question the architect's design expertise if that was the way the building was supposed to look. Everyone laughed because they knew that they couldn't judge how the stadium looked before the building process was finished.

In the same way, let me close this book with a great theological truth: God is not done yet. We may look at our lives and question God's plan and design, but we can rest assured that he is not finished with us yet!

We see this same point time and time again as we read the Bible. God wasn't done when Joseph was in prison, when Jeremiah was in the pit, or when Jonah was in the fish. He wasn't done when Shadrach, Meshach, and Abednego were thrown into the fiery furnace, or when Daniel was cast into the lion's den. He wasn't done when Pharaoh was oppressing the Israelites, when Haman was plotting against Mordecai, when Herod was killing infants, or when Saul was persecuting Christians. He wasn't done when Sarah's womb was barren, when Ruth was a widow, or when the Virgin Mary was told she would bear a son. He was not done when Naaman had leprosy, when Bartimaeus was blind, or when Lazarus was dead. He was not done when Noah built an ark, when Aaron made a golden calf, or when David took a census. He was not done when Goliath taunted the armies of Israel, when Jezebel killed the prophets of Israel, or when the Babylonians destroyed the temple of Israel.

And do not forget that he was not done when Jesus was rejected by his hometown, betrayed by Judas, deserted by his disciples, denied by Peter, tried by the Sanhedrin, condemned by Pilate, mocked by the soldiers, nailed to the cross, and buried in the tomb.

What more evidence do we need? God is not done with us. It does not matter where we are or where we have been—God is not done. Take heart! Don't merely look to the things that are temporary; look to the things that are unseen and eternal.

It does not matter where we are or where we have been—God is not done. Take heart!

What will our lives look like when God fulfills his plans and finishes his work in us? We do not even have an idea of how great it will be. Our wildest imaginations and loftiest expectations fall short. Hope says, "I do not yet know what it will look like when that day comes, but I know that the day is coming—and it will be better than anything I can imagine."

I can hardly wait. I am finished, but God is not. In Jesus's name, press on and don't lose heart.

NOTES

Introduction

1. Rick Reilly, "Worth the Wait," *Sports Illustrated*, October 20, 2003, 81.

2. If you or someone you know struggles with depression, a good place to start would be John Piper, *When the Darkness Will Not Lift: Doing What We Can While We Wait for God—and Joy* (Wheaton: Crossway, 2006).

Chapter 1 What to Do When You Feel Overwhelmed

1. John Piper, "Let All Who Seek Thee Rejoice and Be Glad in Thee; Let Those Who Love Thy Salvation Say Continually, 'The Lord Be Magnified,'" *desiringGod*, from a sermon preached on March 17, 1996, https://www.desiringgod.org/messages/let-all-who-seek-thee-rejoice-and-be-glad-in-thee-let-those-who-love-thy-salvation-say-continually-the-lord-be-magnified.

2. Piper, "Let All Who Seek."

3. "How much water is there on, in, and above the Earth?" *United States Geological Survey*, accessed September 14, 2016, water.usgs.gov/edu/earthhowmuch.html.

4. "The Wild File" *Outside*, January 5, 2003, https://www.outsideonline.com/1821526/wild-file.

5. Helen H. Lemmel, "Turn Your Eyes Upon Jesus," 1922, public domain.

Chapter 2 What to Do When You Feel Defeated

1. Ruth Alexander, "Are there really 100,000 new Christian martyrs every year?" *BBC News*, November 12, 2013, https://www.bbc.com/news/magazine-24864587.

2. Sam Storms, "A Dozen Things God Did with Our Sin," devotional message shared with Bethlehem College and Seminary, December 8, 2016.

3. Iain H. Murray, *D. M. Lloyd-Jones: The Fight of Faith 1939–1981* (Carlisle, PA: Banner of Truth, 1990), 738.

Chapter 3 What to Do When You Feel Worthless

1. J. I. Packer, *Keep in Step with the Spirit* (Grand Rapids: Baker Books, 2005), 57.

2. Professor Andy Bilson, "The Babies Who Suffer in Silence: How Overseas Orphanages Are Damaging Children," *The Telegraph*, November 6, 2017, https://www.telegraph.co.uk/health-fitness/body/babies-suffer-silence-overseas-orphanages-damaging-children/.

3. J. I. Packer, *Knowing God* (Downers Grove, IL: InterVarsity, 1988), 230; emphasis in original.

Chapter 4 What to Do When the Past Paralyzes You

1. Horatio G. Spafford, "It Is Well with My Soul," 1873, public domain.

2. C. S. Lewis, *Mere Christianity* (New York: Touchstone, 1996), 104.

3. Clinton E. Arnold, ed., *Zondervan Illustrated Bible Backgrounds Commentary*, vol. 1: *Matthew, Mark, Luke* (Grand Rapids: Zondervan, 2002), 115.

4. The ESV Global Study Bible®, ESV® Bible (Wheaton, IL: Crossway, 2012), note on Matthew 18:24, https://www.esv.org/Matthew+18/. All rights reserved.

5. This concept has been attributed to many different people. The earliest significant match appears in Bert Ghezzi, *The Angry Christian:*

How to Control and Use Your Anger (Ann Arbor, MI: Servant, 1980), 99. "Resentment is like a poison we carry around inside us with the hope that when we get the chance we can deposit it where it will harm another who has injured us. The fact is that we carry this poison at extreme risk to ourselves."

6. I first heard this language from John Piper, *Future Grace: The Purifying Power of the Promises of God*, rev. ed. (Colorado Springs: Multnomah, 2012), 266. "If you hold a grudge, you doubt the Judge."

Chapter 5 What to Do When the Present Disappoints You

1. D. Martyn Lloyd-Jones, *Setting Our Affections Upon Glory: Nine Sermons on the Gospel and the Church* (Wheaton: Crossway, 2013), 25.

2. Lloyd-Jones, *Setting Our Affections*, 24.

3. Quoted in Thabiti M. Anyabwile, *May We Meet in the Heavenly World: The Piety of Lemuel Haynes* (Grand Rapids: Reformation Heritage Books, 2009), 113.

4. Lewis, *Mere Christianity*, 170.

5. William Cowper, "God Moves in a Mysterious Way," 1774, public domain.

6. Lewis, *Mere Christianity*, 121.

7. C. S. Lewis, *Til We Have Faces* (New York: Harcourt, Brace and Company, 1980), 74–75.

Chapter 6 What to Do When the Future Scares You

1. D. Martyn Lloyd-Jones, *Spiritual Depression* (Grand Rapids: Zondervan, 1965), 265.

2. Lloyd-Jones, *Spiritual Depression*, 264–65.

3. Nik Ripken, *The Insanity of God: A True Story of Faith Resurrected* (Nashville: B&H, 2013), 262–63.

4. John Piper in April of 2009 at a Wednesday night service at Bethlehem Baptist Church in Minneapolis, Minnesota.

ABOUT THE AUTHOR

Jason Meyer is the pastor for preaching and vision at Bethlehem Baptist Church in Minneapolis, Minnesota. He is also an associate professor of preaching at Bethlehem College and Seminary.

The mission statement of his life is the same as the mission statement of his church: "To spread a passion for the supremacy of God in all things for the joy of all peoples through Jesus Christ."

Meyer is the author of *Lloyd-Jones on the Christian Life: Doctrine and Life as Fuel and Fire* (Crossway, 2018); a commentary on Philippians in the ESV Expository Commentary (Crossway, 2018); and *Preaching: A Biblical Theology* (Crossway, 2013). He has also authored a book on the difference in Paul between the old covenant and the new covenant, entitled *The End of the Law: Mosaic Covenant in Pauline Theology* (B&H Academic, 2009).

Jason is head over heels in love with his wife, Cara, and he is the father of four children: Grace, Allie, Jonathan, and David. As a family, the Meyers enjoy camping, hiking, fishing, playing sports, and listening to music.

Connect with **JASON**

© Rick Busch

Follow Jason on social media to keep up with his writing and preaching.